The Lourdes Pilgrim

A Prayerbook & Guide

Oliver Todd

PARACLETE PRESS

BREWSTER, MASSACHUSETTS

Published in the United States in 2006 by Paraclete Press,
Brewster, Massachusetts
www.paracletepress.com
ISBN: 1-55725-494-X
All rights reserved.

First published in Great Britain in 1997 by:
Matthew James Publishing Ltd,
19 Wellington Close,
Chelmsford Essex CM1 2EE
www.matthew-james.co.uk

This revised edition was first published in 2003

Compilation, texts and commentaries © 1997, 2003 Oliver Todd

Printed in China for Compass Press Ltd

4

"PENANCE, PENANCE, PENANCE"

5

"PRAY FOR SINNERS"

INTRODUCTION

In the six years since this book was written, Lourdes has continued to grow and develop, still offering a focus of devotion for millions of pilgrims each year. This revised edition includes the main changes that have taken place and supplies more up to date information on the sites, timetables, contacts and devotional practices. It tells the story of Lourdes, gives an indication of what is to be seen and done there today, and provides liturgical and devotional material to enable the pilgrim to take part in the daily celebrations.

Part One looks at the phenomenon of Lourdes. It recalls the history of the apparitions and of the Church's attitude to Lourdes, and offers some hints on how to get the most out of a pilgrimage.

Part Two is a mini-Gazetteer. It seeks to answer those questions most often asked by the visitor, and to provide information on the daily events in the life of Lourdes. Places of local interest are given, as well as suggestions for anyone wishing to venture further afield in the Pyrénées.

The sacraments most closely associated with Lourdes are given in Part Three: Eucharist, Penance and Anointing of the Sick. Here, as throughout the book, this material is intended to supplement rather than replace whatever has been arranged by organized pilgrimages.

Communal and private prayer forms the contents of Part Four. An outline is also given of the two daily public acts of worship: the Blessed Sacrament Procession and the Marian Celebration (Torchlight Procession).

The final section, Part Five, offers a wide selection of devotional material, including prayers taken from Christian tradition, and a necessarily eclectic selection of hymns and songs.

Thanks are due to those at home and in Lourdes who offered suggestions and corrections to the contents of this book. They are too numerous to be named here, but their contribution has been indispensable. Any errors will be corrected in future editions.

It is my hope that those who use this book will experience that growth in faith and deeper belonging to Christ's Church which is the promise and goal of Lourdes.

Oliver Todd
11th February 2003
Feast of Our Lady of Lourdes

PART ONE

"I AM THE IMMACULATE CONCEPTION"

The Story of Bernadette

The Apparitions

The Message of Lourdes

The Verdict of the Church

Cures

Making a Pilgrimage

QUE SOY
ERA
IMMACULADA COUCEPCIOU

THE STORY OF BERNADETTE

Lourdes, in the middle of the nineteenth century, was a small garrison town of perhaps four or five thousand inhabitants. Nestling at an altitude of about 420 metres in the foothills of the Pyrénées, it was dominated by its fortress or castle, a symbol of its military connections. In fact, for two periods of over fifty years in the thirteenth and fourteenth centuries, Lourdes was occupied by English forces. Like many similar places in this part of the world, it was served by a swift mountain river, the Gave, which passed through the town on its westward route towards Pau, and all in all, apart from its picturesque natural surroundings, it was a most unremarkable place. It had its own parish church and convent, a mayor and council, a hospital, a local newspaper, and a work force which consisted principally of farmers and of marble and slate quarry workers.

It was in this town that François Soubirous and Louise Casterot had set up their home. They married on January 9th 1843, when he was thirty-five years old and she was only nineteen years old. François was a miller and he went to live with his wife's family and to work at the Boly Mill in Lourdes.

A year later, on January 7th 1844, their first child was born, a daughter who was baptized two days later in the Parish Church and given the name of Marie-Bernarde, although she was always known as Bernadette. Madame Soubirous was to give birth eventually to nine children, of whom four boys and one girl would die before reaching the age of ten.

Due to an accident, in November 1844, during which Madame Soubirous was burned when her blouse caught fire from a lighted taper, she was unable to continue breast-feeding Bernadette. So Bernadette was sent to Bartrès, a couple of miles outside of Lourdes, where she stayed for about a year and a half to be wet-nursed by Marie Aravant Lagüe, who acted as her foster mother.

Bernadette's father proved not to be the best of business managers, and things went from bad to worse at the mill. In 1852 the mill was sold, although the Soubirous family had thought that they owned the property. By 1854 François could no longer meet the bills and the family was evicted from the mill. They found accommodation for a while in what today is Rue Bernadette Soubirous.

Worse was to follow. In 1855 Lourdes was attacked by an outbreak of cholera, and Bernadette fell victim to the epidemic. Although she recovered, she developed asthma and tuberculosis, sicknesses which were to remain with her for life.

As their fortunes plunged, the Soubirous family moved from one dwelling to another in an attempt to keep a roof over their heads. They moved away to a mill in Arcizac-ès-Angles, then back to Lourdes where they lodged at the present-day Rue du Bourg. In 1857 they found themselves in the direst of straits and ended up living in one tiny room of the Cachot, a rotting and disused prison on Rue des Petits Fossés. Their situation was aggravated when in that same year François, unemployed and destitute, was thrown into prison for a week, allegedly for stealing a sack of flour.

While the family tried to exist at the Cachot, Bernadette, who once more was ill, went back to her foster mother in Bartrès, where she acted as a shepherdess. With the scant education that had been afforded her, she could neither read nor write. This meant that she had also missed her formal religious education and was now at the age when she would normally make her First Communion, but she knew little catechism.

In January 1858 Bernadette returned to Lourdes and began preparation with the Sisters of Nevers for her First Communion. She attended their free classes, but because she was illiterate, she was taught with children who were many years younger than her.

Within a month of returning in 1858, she saw the eighteen apparitions of the Virgin Mary. A full chronicle of what took place during these is given elsewhere.

On June 3rd 1858, at the age of fourteen and just over a month before the final apparition, Bernadette made her First Communion with the rest of her class in the Hospital Chapel in Lourdes.

Bernadette began to be visited by groups of pilgrims who now came to Lourdes, but despite her poverty she refused to accept any gifts or money saying, "I prefer to remain poor." The parish priest, Fr Peyramale, found an alternative home for the Soubirous family who moved out of the Cachot. During this time Bernadette was under continual scrutiny from those authorities who sought to discredit the story of the apparitions and the message of the Virgin Mary. Her constant reply to this was, "It is not my job to make you believe it; I am charged only with the task of telling it to you."

Early in 1860 Bernadette was confirmed by Bishop Laurence of Tarbes, in whose diocese Lourdes is situated. Later that same year she went to school as a boarder with the nuns in Lourdes. She was small for her age, about 1.40m (4ft 7in), extremely playful despite being sickly, and soon began to read and write, as well as developing her skills at needlework. She stayed with the nuns for the next six years, and it was whilst she was there, on January 18th 1862, that the Church authorities declared the apparitions to be true and work on building a church was begun.

During this period, as she hosted more and more pilgrims who began to descend on Lourdes, she began to consider whether she was being called by God to a religious vocation. Two things hampered her: her continual sickness and her lack of a dowry. The Bishop of Nevers, Mgr Forcade, agreed to admit her to the congregation of the convent at Nevers despite having no dowry to offer, and after much thought and prayer interspersed by bouts of ill health, she left Lourdes for the Congregation of the Sisters of Nevers on July 3rd 1866.

Bernadette took Simple Vows on October 30th 1867, having reverted to her true baptismal name as Sister Marie-

Bernarde. She considered it her duty to perform in the convent surroundings the works of prayer and penance that Our Lady had asked of her. She looked after the sick sisters as infirmarian until 1873 and was renowned for her ability to be cheerful in her duties, even though she herself did not enjoy good health. For a short while she worked as sacristan in 1874, but by 1875 she was mostly confined to the infirmary as a seriously ill patient.

Her Perpetual Vows were made on September 22nd 1878. She struggled with respiratory problems: asthma and coughing-up blood. In addition she developed a tumour on her right knee.

On Wednesday April 16th 1879 the nuns gathered round her bed and she joined them in prayer. In the course of these prayers she died, aged thirty-five years.

She was beatified by Pope Pius XI on 14th June 1925, and canonized by him on 8th December 1933. Today she is honoured as a saint not because the Virgin Mary appeared to her, but because of the holiness which she showed throughout her life and particularly in her final thirteen years at the convent.

THE EIGHTEEN APPARITIONS

1: Thursday 11th February 1858

Bernadette went to collect firewood with her sister Toinette-Marie (11yrs) and a friend, Jeanne Abadie (13yrs). Whilst the other two went across a small stream, the Savy Canal, Bernadette paused to take off her stockings. She heard a gust of wind, but the trees remained still. She looked towards the nearby grotto of Massabielle and saw a lady dressed in a white dress with a blue sash. The lady had a yellow rose in each foot which matched the colour of her rosary chain. Bernadette copied the lady in making the sign of the cross and praying the Rosary. As soon as she had finished the Rosary the vision disappeared. Neither of the other two girls saw the vision.

2: Sunday 14th February 1858

Along with some other children Bernadette returned to the grotto. She persuaded her mother to let her go, and she collected some holy water from the church to take with her. When the lady appeared, Bernadette threw the holy water at the vision, believing that if the vision was from God then all would be well, and if from elsewhere then the holy water would make the lady go away. The more Bernadette threw the water, the more the lady smiled. But still the vision remained silent.

3: Thursday 18th February 1858

The day after Ash Wednesday, accompanied now by several important people from the town, Bernadette saw the vision once more and asked the lady to put in writing whatever she had to say. Declining this request, the lady spoke instead. She asked Bernadette if she would come to the grotto every day for a fortnight. She also told Bernadette that she did not promise to make her happy in this world, but in the next.

4: *Friday 19th February 1858*

Bernadette went this time with her mother to the grotto of Massabielle, and the lady appeared, but only Bernadette saw her.

5: *Saturday 20th February 1858*

Yet again Bernadette visited the grotto with her mother where the lady appeared for the fifth time but did not speak.

6: *Sunday 21st February 1858*

As crowds began to follow Bernadette to the rock of the grotto, the lady appeared to her, giving her the message to pray for sinners. Bernadette was seen to be in tears during this apparition.

7: *Tuesday 23rd February 1858*

Although Bernadette was keeping her promise to visit each day for a fortnight, the lady did not appear on the Monday. Nevertheless, Bernadette returned on the Tuesday when the seventh apparition took place amid prayer and silence. By now there were about 250 people who came to the grotto in the hope of seeing what Bernadette saw.

8: *Wednesday 24th February 1858*

On this day the lady appeared and told Bernadette to pray for the conversion of sinners, a message she would repeat several times in the future. She asked Bernadette to get on her knees and kiss the ground in penance for sinners. This was the first time she used the word "penance".

9: *Thursday 25th February 1858*

The lady spoke again to Bernadette, ordering her to eat the grass which was there and to go to the spring where she was to take a drink and wash herself. Mistakenly thinking that the lady meant the river, Bernadette went towards the River Gave. The lady directed her under the rock of the grotto where she found a dirty patch of water. She scratched the ground a few times before being able to get water clean enough to drink.

10: Saturday 27th February 1858

There was no apparition on the Friday, but on the Saturday Bernadette saw the lady once more and continued the penitential practices that had been requested of her.

11: Sunday 28th February 1858

The eleventh apparition took place with the lady repeating the message she had given earlier about the need for prayer and penance.

12: Monday 1st March 1858

The lady was seen yet again by Bernadette, although she did not speak. By now the story of what was happening in Lourdes had spread and on this day there were in excess of a thousand people surrounding the grotto.

13: Tuesday 2nd March 1858

When Bernadette went to the grotto the lady gave her two commands. She was to go to the priests and tell them that people should come to the place in procession. She was also to say that a chapel should be built there. By now Bernadette was coming under severe scrutiny by the local clergy who demanded to know the name of the lady.

14: Wednesday 3rd March 1858

Having had no vision in the morning, Bernadette went back in the afternoon and saw the lady who repeated her request of the previous day regarding the chapel. The local priest demanded that Bernadette ask some sort of miraculous sign from the lady as proof of the apparition.

15: Thursday 4th March 1858

On the last day of the fortnight's visits there were about 7,000 people who gathered for the apparition. When Bernadette asked the lady for her name, she merely smiled.

16: Thursday 25th March 1858

Three weeks later, on the feast of the Annunciation, Bernadette asked the lady her name three times and received only a smile in reply. After the fourth time the lady spoke, using the local dialect of Bernadette, and said, "I am the Immaculate Conception".

17: *Wednesday 7th April 1858*

The silent apparition lasted for about an hour, and in front of several hundred people Bernadette went into such a deep ecstasy that the flame of a candle burned on her fingers for about fifteen minutes without leaving any trace of a mark.

18: *Friday 16th July 1858*

The grotto had now been barricaded by the authorities, but from the meadow opposite the River Gave Bernadette saw the lady for the last time. On this feast of Our Lady of Mount Carmel, she said nothing. But Bernadette commented that she looked more radiant and beautiful than ever.

Bernadette also reported that during the course of the fortnight's visits (18th February-4th March), the lady passed on three secrets to her which she was not to disclose to anybody.

THE MESSAGE OF LOURDES

Today, when Lourdes is internationally known and when the town has mushroomed into a centre of pilgrimage, commerce and tourism, it is essential to peel off its outer skins in order to see the real purpose of Lourdes. Otherwise we run the risk of seeing only what Lourdes does, rather than perceiving what Lourdes is. Getting behind the external appearances and the flurry of activities, we need to ask what is the true message of Lourdes.

✠ What is it about the apparitions to Bernadette that has enduring significance?

✠ What must we not lose sight of if we are to be faithful to the spiritual experience?

✠ How can we reap the deeper benefits of this place of pilgrimage?

✠ What is God, through Mary and Bernadette, trying to tell us in this place as the third millennium begins?

The message of Lourdes is a simple one. It takes no genius to understand it. It is the same message that we can find in the pages of the gospel, if we take time to look. It brings no new teaching, no startling revelations or magical promises, but simply calls us once more back to the basics of the good news of Jesus. It can be summed up in four simple ideas:

✠ **Poverty**

✠ **Prayer**

✠ **Penance**

✠ **Participation**

The jigsaw of Lourdes is incomplete without each of these four pieces, and when we put them all together we find the heart of the message and the source of its inspiration: the gospel. To heed the message of Lourdes is to return to the word of God.

✠ Poverty

God makes a habit of picking those whom we would not consider to be the obvious choice. Time and time again in the Bible we see God choosing the underdog to be a leader, a prophet or an apostle. Those who appear to have all the qualifications seem to be left aside as God puts a seal of approval on someone weak or lowly, someone whom the world considers of little significance.

So Moses becomes the mouthpiece of God, even though he had a speech impediment; David overcomes the giant Goliath; the young boy Jeremiah is chosen to be a disturbing prophet; Mary, the virgin, becomes the mother of God and the volatile Peter is placed at the head of the apostles.

What the Lord looks for is not the outward appearance, but the inner quality. It is poverty of spirit, or true humility, which is pleasing to God. It is this humility that Jesus himself models for us:

> *"...though he was in the form of God, he did not regard equality with God as something to be exploited, but emptied himself, taking the form of a slave, being born in human likeness. And being found in human form, he humbled himself and became obedient to the point of death - even death on a cross."* (Philippians 2:6-8)

True poverty of spirit does not mean that we deny our gifts and talents. It means, rather, that we acknowledge where they come from - God. It means being open to the word of God, listening for the call God makes to us, and responding with a generosity of heart which seeks not our own advancement but the glory of God.

Such poverty is reflected in the life of Bernadette, in her family background and in her trusting response in faith to what was revealed by the Virgin Mary. Today it is reflected in the very ambience of Lourdes: the simplicity of the sites, the noble yet uncomplicated style of public worship, the accessibility of its music and prayer.

It calls us back to the simple Christian life where our true wealth lies not in things and possessions but in the way we care for the sick and disabled, those on the margins of our society, those who lack political or social justice, and those whose lives are torn apart by war, violence and oppression.

"I do not promise you happiness in this world," said Mary to Bernadette, "but in the other."

The message of poverty challenges us to name our true wealth.

✠ Prayer

If we have the right dispositions, then all our pilgrimage, from the moment we set out from home until our return there, can be one great act of prayer. Alternatively it could be nothing more than a religious holiday.

Prayer is not simply about words that we say silently or out loud. It is more to do with what is in our hearts. Prayer of the heart goes beyond mere formulas (although these can be helpful) to a dedication of our whole selves to God through our thoughts, words and actions.

Hence, pushing a wheelchair can be prayer; singing at liturgy can be prayer; listening sensitively to someone at table can be prayer; taking time to socialize with other pilgrims is not just time off from God, but can be genuine prayer.

Jesus warns us about confusing words with prayer, since they are not the same:

> "When you are praying, do not heap up empty phrases as the Gentiles do; for they think that they will be heard because of their many words. Do not be like them, for your Father knows what you need before you ask him " (Matthew 6:7-8)

Of course, there is nothing wrong with set prayers like the Rosary, Litanies, Acts of Contrition etc. We could never pray together unless we had some common set forms that everyone knew. But what the message of Lourdes is asking of us is that we go beyond the words and make our lives an act of prayer. The prayer of Lourdes is about a heart to heart listening to what God is asking of us at this time in our lives.

The reports of the apparitions make it clear that Bernadette did not spend all her time chattering to Mary. There was a communion between the two of them, a dialogue of hearts which did not always need words. Our pilgrimage will succeed if we learn to treasure those moments, cither alone or in prayer with others, when we become acutely aware of God's presence and are able to offer him praise just for being our God and for bothering to have us as his sons and daughters.

This prayer can catch hold of us at any time of day, at the Grotto or in a cafe, in silence or in song, alone or with others. For Christians it is only this type of prayer which ultimately can make sense of our lives. We do not only pray that everything will turn out well in heaven; we pray to make sense of our lives now. This prayer needs to be intimate, personal and honest.

We have all promised to pray for others during our visit to Lourdes. The best way to do this is not simply with prayers, but with a life of prayer.

The message of prayer challenges us to make our daily actions an offering to God.

☦ Penance

If penance were nothing more than certain actions which caused us inconvenience and irritation, then religion would be easy to practise. Wearing a hair shirt, going without food and drink, crawling on our knees - all of these would be a quick way into the kingdom of heaven.

Such acts of penance were known to Bernadette who crawled like a pig in the dirt as a result of one of the apparitions. They were familiar also to Jesus who suffered mockery, insult and physical violence on his way to Calvary:

"When he was abused, he did not return abuse; when he suffered, he did not threaten; but he entrusted himself to the one who judges justly. He himself bore our sins in his body on the cross, so that, free from sins, we might live for righteousness; by his wounds you have been healed." (I Peter 2:23-24)

Most of us have our own particular penances that we carry through life. For some it is sickness, for others bereavement, and for many it is a sense of rejection or disappointment that we bear silently. We have no shortage of things to try us.

The penance of the gospel, and of Mary's message to Bernadette, goes beyond even these trials. It is a penance of mind and body, a conversion of heart, a return to the God who loves us. We do not use penitential practices simply as an ascetic way to punish our bodies, but as a reminder to us of what we stand to lose if we let sin come between us and our God.

This discipline of mind, or conversion, was Mary's call to Bernadette to do penance for sinners. To wash herself with the water from the spring and to drink from it was a sign of her own need to be cleansed and refreshed by the message of the gospel.

Knowing our sinfulness and trying constantly to walk on a path of conversion and repentance is what true penance is about. It involves a change of heart, an acknowledgement that what I am is less than what God wants me to be. And so the acts of penance which I undertake are of value only insofar as they reflect my inner intention of coming closer to God.

My penance can also affect others. I can pray for sinners, and the example of my own conversion can have consequences for other people. If, like the father of the prodigal son, I am aware of the loss which sin can cause, then I am in a position to feel compassion and solidarity with those whose sin has left them impoverished. I also realize that my sin has injured the Body of Christ, the other members of the Church.

This compassion, brought on by penance for my own sin, leads me to pray for sinners, since they are my own Christian flesh and blood. Penance, then, is not simply an individual thing between me and God; it is an attitude and action of the whole Church.

The message of penance challenges us to renew our baptismal commitment to turn away from whatever keeps us from God.

✠ Participation

Even people who may be shy or reticent back home seem to have no difficulty in joining in things at Lourdes. They participate often at a deeper level than in their own parishes.

This vocal, active participation foreshadows something more fundamental, something which Mary asked of Bernadette and which the gospel demands of every one of us who is baptized: participation in the mission and life of the Church.

When Mary spoke about building a church and getting people to come to Lourdes in procession, it was understood at face value. Its results can be seen daily in the Domaine.

But the type of participation in the message of Lourdes, the type of building which has to be done, goes beyond bricks and mortar, beyond joining in processions and singing hymns, to a full and active participation in building up the Body of Christ:

> *"So with yourselves; since you are eager for spiritual gifts, strive to excel in them for building up the Church."* (I Cor 14:12)

This means recognizing that the real pilgrimage is that of the Pilgrim People of God: the Church. It means that participation in a pilgrimage to Lourdes is not a end in itself but a beginning.

To take part in all the activities in Lourdes is to sign up for a commitment when we get back home. For as we move around the Domaine in the Torchlight Procession or follow the Blessed Sacrament into the Esplanade, we are implicitly accepting that as baptized members of the Church we have a part to play in its mission.

To participate in the liturgies means that in the life of the Church we cannot be spectators. Each of us has been graced by the Holy Spirit with the dignity of a full member of God's people. Building up the Church is the task we have when we return to our own countries, to our homes, to our families and friends.

The gospel asks us not to worship God with our mouths if our hearts are far from him. Coming to Lourdes means that we take this seriously. Pilgrimages are not fringe events to pass our leisure time pleasantly. Far from being hobbies for the godly, they are demanding occasions. They demand that the Church to which we make appeal while in Lourdes, is the same Church that we agree to build up when we get home.

The message of participation challenges us to take our full place in the Church whose song we sing.

Poverty of spirit, prayer from the heart, penance of mind and body, and participation in the life of the Church are the heart of Mary's message to Bernadette at Lourdes. These four things are noteworthy in that they have formed part of the core teaching of the Church since its beginnings. In this way the message of Lourdes calls us back to the gospel, and invites us through our prayers, processions and penance to return to Jesus.

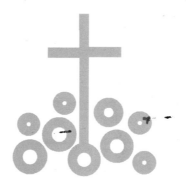

THE VERDICT OF THE CHURCH

To understand what the Church has to say about the events of Lourdes we need to look back to the nineteenth century and then forward to the present day.

It was clear at the time of the apparitions, and immediately afterwards, that there were people who suspected the whole story to be concocted. At worst it was a plot and at best it was a delusion. An often stated opinion was that it was a trick on the part of Bernadette or the priests.

After an exhaustive enquiry which lasted more than four years, the bishop of Tarbes announced on 18th January 1862:

"We judge that the Immaculate Mary, Mother of God, really appeared to Bernadette Soubirous...that this apparition shows all the characteristics of truth and that those who accept it are well-founded in sure belief."

The truthfulness of Bernadette was later accepted implicitly when she was beatified and canonized. This means that the judgement of the local Church, regarding the character and motives of Bernadette, was given universal approval by the actions of Pope Pius XI.

But the Church does not demand that we believe the events of Lourdes as part of our faith. The only person who can ever be held in conscience bound to believe this is Bernadette herself. Lourdes is not an article of faith, far from it. If the events of Lourdes had never taken place, then it would not change the teaching of the Church one iota.

However, the Church proclaims forcefully that what Lourdes is about today, is consonant with the teachings of Christ and worthy of imitation. It says that the message of Lourdes is yet another echo, reinforcement and restatement of the gospel precepts. Poverty, penance, prayer and participation are all practices which build up the Body of Christ. They spring out of the gospel and are at the heart of the Lourdes experience.

Today, more than ever, Lourdes is accepted as being part of the mainstream of Catholic tradition. In trying to discern the contemporary role of Lourdes in the Christian life, the Church keeps a number of factors in mind:

✠ Lourdes is about Christ. Devotion to Mary is ultimately devotion to Christ whose grace has triumphed in Mary. The apparitions do not stop at Mary; they are transparent, letting us see through to what Jesus is saying to us.

✠ The message of Lourdes is rooted in the message of the gospel. It echoes the evangelists' teaching whilst never claiming parity of importance with the gospel. The true spirit of Lourdes calls us back to a deeper appreciation of the word of God.

✠ Lourdes steers clear of making magical claims. It maintains our individual cooperation with Christ in all things, respecting human dignity and divine purpose. It makes no promises of easy grace and remains subservient to the the sovereignty of God and the freedom of human action.

✠ Mary is presented positively as the highest honour of our race. She is not portrayed as a redeemer or mediator, for there is only one – Jesus Christ. She is put forward as a created member of the Church, as a model of discipleship and as herself one of the redeemed.

✠ Any tendency to mere individual piety is contradicted by Lourdes. Lourdes constantly recalls us to the fact that we are a Pilgrim People of God, to the community or ecclesial dimension of our faith. We act not only as individuals but as Church, and we share a communion with those saints who have gone before us.

✠ There is nothing in the message of Lourdes which denies, contradicts, exaggerates or gives undue attention to any aspect of the Church's teaching. Rather, it calls us to wholeness and to that Christian unity which is the fruit of communal prayer and worship.

So today the Church encourages pilgrimages to Lourdes and expresses the hope that those who undertake them will reap the benefits of spiritual renewal. Just as Mary and Bernadette were both transformed by the power of God's grace, so too we hope that our time in Lourdes may be a graced period for us and for our fellow pilgrims.

CURES

Each year many people come to Lourdes hoping for a cure. We know that to be cured can mean many things. The best cure is a change of heart, a renewed commitment to hear God's word, like Mary, and to give our joyful assent of "yes" to what God asks of us. This takes us from the disease of sin to the ease of Christ's yoke. Such a cure is open to anyone who has ears to hear God speaking in Lourdes.

At other times people receive a healing which takes them from the spiritual doldrums into a more vibrant relationship with God. Some people experience, through prayer and friendship with others, a deeper sense of belonging to the Body of Christ, a moral renewal, or a growth in hope that Lourdes gives them. This freshness of life is another word for grace.

Thousands of people come to Lourdes each year hoping that some sickness which they have, either mental or physical, might be lifted from them, or at least eased. They are seeking a medical cure.

There is no shortage of evidence that medical cures take place at Lourdes. But before such healing can be considered miraculous, there are three conditions which have to be met:

✠ It must be demonstrated that the illness actually existed

✠ There must be proper evidence that the cure took place

✠ Natural causes must be ruled out

The Medical Bureau in Lourdes is the body which looks into the various claims for miraculous cures. Although it is a permanent body, it enjoys the collaboration of numerous doctors and medical scientists from throughout the world, both Christians and non-Christians, believers and non-believers alike. Before a case can be referred to the Church authorities, the Bureau has to satisfy itself beyond doubt that there is no medical explanation for what has occurred.

It takes several years to investigate cases such as these, since complete medical observation and documentation is required over a period of time so that the medical professionals can be as circumspect as possible. Doctors are aware that symptoms of recovery could be due to purely natural or pharmacological reasons. Sometimes a person appears to have been cured but is simply in a prolonged period of clinical remission. An improvement does not mean a cure, and a cure does not mean a miracle.

When the Medical Bureau has decided that the cure is a "phenomenon contrary to the observations and experience of medical knowledge, and scientifically inexplicable", it passes its findings on to the International Medical Committee of Lourdes, which is made up of some of the highest medical and scientific authorities from universities, hospitals and medical academies throughout the world.

If the International Medical Committee ratifies the Bureau's findings, then the whole dossier is sent to the bishop of the diocese from which the patient came. It is the bishop who weighs all the claims of the case, and, with his local knowledge of the faith and circumstances of the person involved, finally declares the cure to be miraculous or otherwise. Since the beginning there have been thousands of cures, but only about 70 have been classed as miraculous.

When Jesus worked miracles of healing during his lifetime it was not as a performance or trick. The miracle was never an end in itself, although it often brought great relief to the person who was cured. Rather, it was as a sign of his authority and the truthfulness of his claims that he cured people. Miracles were signs that he was indeed the Son of God. The pity which Jesus felt for the crowd or for certain individuals was an indication that he had come to free us from the hold that sin and death can have over us. The miracle was only a deposit, a down-payment on what he really was offering: eternal life now and to come.

This gift of Jesus, this grace of God, is freely available to all who seek it sincerely. It is readily seen in the cures of mind, body, soul and spirit experienced by many of the five million people who visit Lourdes each year.

MAKING A PILGRIMAGE

When the persecutions of the Church were ended in the early fourth century, and the Emperor Constantine was baptized, the Christians came out from the underground, free at last from fear of reprisal and death. Their religion was no longer illegal and they began to practise their faith openly, with many of them travelling to places connected with the life of Jesus. When Constantine's mother, the Empress Helena, visited Jerusalem in 326 AD, the era of the Christian pilgrimage had begun.

Some fascinating records survive of these pilgrimages at first undertaken usually by individuals rather than groups. By pure coincidence, the first substantial evidence of such a journey comes from an unnamed man, living not too far from Lourdes, who visited Palestine in 333. He is called the Bordeaux Pilgrim and he leaves us a very full travelogue of his journey from France to the Holy Land.

A little later in the same century we have an account of a similar journey undertaken from 381-384 by a woman named Egeria. It is likely that she was either from the Atlantic coast in modern-day northern Spain or a Gaul from Aquitaine in modern-day France. She was probably a nun and she leaves us a useful account of how the liturgical year was celebrated in those days, besides giving an insight into the cultural life of the Middle East.

With the passing of time pilgrimages began to increase in popularity, and as the Christian faith spread so did the number of holy places throughout Christendom that were visited by pilgrims. A particular favourite was Rome, where people went to visit the tombs of the apostles Peter and Paul.

Pilgrimages were undertaken as a sign of devotion and as an expiation for sins; indeed, in the middle ages, making a pilgrimage was often the penance given to a person who went to confession. As the number of pilgrims increased, pilgrimages began to be organized on a grand scale. Chaucer immortalized the characters on their way to St Thomas Becket's tomb at Canterbury in England, while in western Europe the most famous pilgrimage trail led to Compostela in Spain where the shrine of St James is situated.

Since pilgrimages seem to be a constant feature of religious practice, Christian and non-Christian (eg. Muslims who visit Mecca), we can reasonably ask, What are they for? Why do people go on them? and How can we get the most from them?

Very soon we come up with the answer that what takes place on a pilgrimage, what it is all about, is a microcosm of our life's response to God's call of faith. Compressed into a small space of time, a pilgrimage is a reflection of our life's journey towards God, with all the decisions and demands that this makes on us. On a pilgrimage which might last only a week, we encounter the spiritual milestones of our lifetime's journey in faith.

A pilgrimage is:

✚ **a journey**

✚ **towards God**

✚ **with a purpose**

A Journey

A pilgrimage is a journey with a difference. It is more than a journey undertaken just for the sake of travel. It is a journey undertaken for the sake of faith.

It would be possible to take a religious holiday or vacation and to visit all the famous cathedrals of Europe. This pleasant trip would be fine; it might teach us a lot about God, the Church and society, but it would not be a pilgrimage.

What turns a journey into a pilgrimage is the reason why we embark upon it, and the intention we have in carrying it out. We have come on a pilgrimage to Lourdes because by so doing we are able to profess publicly our desire to come closer to God and to discipline ourselves by prayer and penance.

In former times, before trains and planes, part of the penance consisted in the actual journey itself, which was often difficult and dangerous. Today that is less of a problem.

To be a pilgrim, and not just a tourist, I must undertake this journey as a sign that I want to strengthen my faith.

Towards God

Every journey has a destination, and pilgrimages have as their destinations places which are significant, which are holy, which are renowned for bringing us closer to God.

Wherever God's Spirit blows, people gather as pilgrims. This can be on the top of mountains, in desert places, in caves or in ancient religious sites. Finding God is really more important than finding the pilgrimage destination. In fact, we can say that God is the true destination of any Christian pilgrimage.

What makes a place holy is not some sort of incense which hangs over it. Rather, a place is made holy by the holiness of the lives of those who struggle to reach it. Lourdes is remarkable because the Virgin Mary appeared there. It is even more remarkable today for the sight of thousands of people from every corner of the globe who come, often with great personal sacrifice, to express their faith in God and in the promises made to them by Jesus, God's son.

In this public journey towards God we are not alone. We are strengthened and supported by the faith of those who journey with us. We are encouraged by the forebearance of the sick, by the patience of those who nurse them, by the friendship of those who are fellow travellers with us on our journey. In their faces we are drawn nearer to a place of grace, where we might glimpse yet a new aspect of the face of God. For it is God we have come to see.

With a purpose

It is perfectly alright to enjoy the holiday aspects of a pilgrimage. Pilgrimages do not have to be dismal affairs;

they are about regeneration and refreshment, about relaxation as well as work. In fact, the fun shared between people on a pilgrimage is often the basis for forming friendships which go on to last for many years to come.

When God called Abraham to leave on a mammoth journey from Ur in the Chaldees to the land which was to be given to his descendants, he asked him to make a great act of faith and to uproot himself from his home surroundings. He was to begin a new life, living in a completely different way than before. If he would do as God asked, then God promised to look after him. His answer to God has earned him the title of "Abraham, our Father in Faith."

God asks a similar thing of us when we make a pilgrimage. Not that we leave for ever our family and friends back home, but that by making this journey we agree to follow wherever God may lead.

The journey we make has a special purpose: that we agree to put aside whatever keeps us from God, and undergo a true conversion of heart and life. It means that we determine to change as a result of this pilgrimage. We undertake to rid ourselves of what is not of God, and together with those who share our pilgrimage we recognize our communal duty to build a world and society in which God reigns.

The sign we give

The Second Vatican Council draws our attention to the sign value of making a pilgrimage. We are looked at by others because of our faith in Jesus Christ:

> *"Those who travel abroad, for international activities, on business, or on holiday, should keep in mind that no matter where they may be, they are the travelling messengers of Christ, and should bear themselves really as such."* (Decree on Apostolate of Lay People, no.14)

This is not intended as a schoolteacher's warning, but as a reminder that pilgrimages are signs of our commitment, and are evangelizing moments for those we encounter during our travels. Anyone who takes part in a pilgrimage is a mini-sacrament of the gospel to the hundreds and thousands of people on the way. We become "travelling messengers of Christ" to those we meet on the route. By being faithful to our pilgrimage ideals we can act as a sign that might point others in the direction of Christ. The way pilgrims conduct themselves is linked with their ability to be Christ to others.

So our coming to Lourdes is:

✠ A journey towards God with a purpose

✠ Responding to the never-ending call to conversion

✠ An invitation to move with others in a constant renewal of ourselves, our Church, our society and our world

✠ The start of a pilgrimage which will last for life

✠ A sign to the world that we are travelling messengers of Christ

✠ A journey which in one week mirrors all the hopes, joys, and fears of a lifetime seeking God

All this, and more, is the challenge of a pilgrimage!

THE PILGRIM'S COMMANDMENTS

✠ Do not feel obliged to attend everything that is on offer each day in Lourdes

✠ Conserve your strength; there is no merit in tiring yourself out

✠ Make the Mass the central activity of your day

✠ If possible, try to celebrate Morning Prayer and Evening Prayer communally with your pilgrimage

✠ Always double-check each day about times and venues for your pilgrimage events

✠ Try not to be late for meals in the hotels

✠ Even if others ignore it, observe the silence around the Domaine and in the churches and chapels

✠ Wherever possible, keep the spirit of the pilgrimage by joining in with others rather than doing things alone

✠ Don't be afraid to participate fully, to pray fervently and to sing from the heart

✠ Enjoy the social occasions with your fellow pilgrims

✠ Pay a visit to the old part of Lourdes and consider a "day off" by taking a tour to a nearby place of interest

✠ Resist the temptation to kill time; it is too precious

✠ Cultivate a "pilgrim mentality" which accepts the minor inconveniences that go with accommodating so many pilgrims

✠ Consider visiting some of the shrines at off-peak times

✠ Remember that no question is silly if you need to ask it

✠ Don't forget that the sick always have priority in Lourdes

A PILGRIM FOR LIFE

John Bunyan is probably best remembered for his book "The Pilgrim's Progress." It chronicles the journey of its hero to his ultimate destiny. All pigrimages are a reflection of the journey of faith we make in life. The commitments we make in our pilgrimage to Lourdes are mirror images of the decisions we have to take over a lifetime. They are about life, death, sickness, pain, love, forgiveness, committment, healing, patience, perseverance, guilt, choices, etc. In a real sense we can say that to be a Christian is to be a pilgrim. The way we live our daily lives should also be " a journey towards God with a purpose."

John Bunyan's theme, that each of us is on a journey to God, is echoed by the famous hymn of recommitment, "To be a Pilgrim" which could be the anthem of anyone making a pilgrimage:

> He who would valiant be 'gainst all disaster,
> let him in constancy follow the Master.
> There's no discouragement shall make him once relent
> his first avowed intent to be a pilgrim.

> Who so beset him round with dismal stories,
> do but themselves confound: his strength the more is.
> No foes shall stay his might though he with giants fight:
> he will make good his right to be a pilgrim.

> Since, Lord, thou dost defend us with thy Spirit,
> we know we at the end shall life inherit.
> Then fancies flee away! I'll fear not what men say,
> I'll labour night and day to be a pilgrim.

Words: Percy Dearmer (1867-1936)
after John Bunyan (1628-88)

PART TWO

"COME HERE IN PROCESSION"

Places of Interest in Lourdes

Locator Map

Seasonal Pilgrimage Timetables

One Day Pilgrims

Useful Words and Phrases

Visiting the Local Area

Touring the Pyrénées

The Pilgrim's A-Z of Lourdes

PLACES OF INTEREST IN LOURDES

The following is a list of some of the places connected with St Bernadette and the apparitions, as well as those buildings which today are used by people on pilgrimage to Lourdes. Other places not mentioned below, and further details of opening times etc., may be found in the Pilgrim's A-Z of Lourdes on pp.68-90, and in the Seasonal Pilgrimage Timetables on pp.52-53.

STATUE OF THE CROWNED VIRGIN

This stands on the edge of Rosary Square at the crossroads of pilgrim routes through the Domaine and is therefore a good rallying point. The statue is 2.50m high and cast in bronze. The set of rosary beads held by the Virgin is of the older Brigittine style, and if you look carefully you can see that it contains six decades.

GROTTO

The Grotto marks the spot in the cave of the rock of Massabielle where St Bernadette saw the Virgin Mary eighteen times in 1858. It is the most sacred of all the sanctuaries in Lourdes, and has been the natural gathering place for millions of pilgrims who have stood there in silent prayer.

An altar has been erected for the celebration of Eucharist, along with a sacristy on the right hand side. The votive candles which burn there constantly are kept in a small storage place close by, and about 800 tonnes of wax is burnt each year.

But the most striking focal point is the statue of the Immaculate Conception which hovers above in the hollow of the rock. It carries the now famous inscription in the local patois, "I am the Immaculate Conception." Under it there is a rose bush which serves as a reminder of the Parish Priest's request that a rose should bloom in February as a sign of the truthfulness of Bernadette's story.

There is a plaque in the pavement on the left hand side which marks where Bernadette stood when first she saw the "beautiful lady". There is a box in which pilgrims put prayer petitions. (Do not put money in envelopes as they are eventually burned.) A walkway allows a constant flow of people to enter into the heart of the Grotto and touch or kiss the rock. Covered by a glass screen and illuminated is the spring which Bernadette uncovered on 25th February 1858. This water is piped from here to the Baths and to the Taps.

Apart from the celebration of the Eucharist, there is TOTAL SILENCE at all times at the Grotto.

BATHS

The Baths (Piscines) are situated just further along from the Grotto. Although there are seventeen of them, there are always long queues in the summer time, particularly for the female section.

The water comes from the spring in the Grotto which at high season can produce up to nine gallons (40litres) per minute. The water is extremely cold, rarely rising above 15C (59F).

Sometimes it happens that the baths have to be reserved for groups of very sick pilgrims who require a long time to make proper use of them. When this happens the normal queues are suspended, and it is very unlikely that the casual caller will be able to take a bath.

CRYPT

The Crypt was the first church to be built in answer to Mary's request, and it was blessed on Pentecost Sunday 1866. Bernadette, whose father had worked on its construction, was present for this ceremony but hidden among the Children of Mary. From that day onwards, pilgrimages officially began.

Situated underneath what is now the Upper Basilica, it is a dark and squat building whose walls, like those of the Upper and Rosary Basilicas, are covered with marble plaques (known as *"ex voto"* plaques) which express thanks to God for favours received. At the entrance of the corridor can be seen a statue of St Peter, and one of Pius X who encouraged frequent communion and communion for children.

UPPER BASILICA

Known by everybody as the Upper Basilica, its real title is the Basilica of the Immaculate Conception, and over the entrance is a mosaic of Pope Pius IX who in 1854 defined the doctrine of the Immaculate Conception. Built over the Crypt, it was consecrated in 1876. There is wheelchair access through the door on Avenue Mgr Théas.

It is a very striking and ambitious building built on the rock of Massabielle and designed in the Gothic style. A chapel stands on either side of the entrance, St Ann to the right and St Joan of Arc to the left. The Sanctuary stands over the very spot where Bernadette saw Mary.

Besides the *"ex voto"* plaques, the walls are covered with pilgrimage banners from around the world. A further fifteen side chapels contain stained glass windows which depict the story of Lourdes, and the clerestory windows above the nave portray Mary as the "Second Eve".

Outside it is the 70 metres high spire which dominates the Domaine. A two tonne bell is one of four which chime every quarter of an hour, and the clock plays the "Ave" on the hour.

ROSARY BASILICA

This is the third of the early buildings of Lourdes, opened in 1889 and consecrated in 1901. It is built against the rock of the Grotto on what is almost ground level, and it will hold about 1,500 people.

On either side of the entrance facade are two medallions. One is of Pope Pius XII who called the Marian Year of 1954, and the other is of Pope Leo XIII, known as the "Rosary Pope". In between these two, over the central door, is a depiction of Mary offering a rosary to St Dominic who is accredited as its founder.

Inside there is an enclosed ecumenical chapel of the Hospitality with some seats and several Ukrainian icons. Around the Church there are fifteen chapels dedicated to the mysteries of the Rosary, beginning on the left. The fifteenth chapel contains mosaics which represent people involved with St Bernadette and the apparitions.

In the upper wall of the Sanctuary there is a large mosaic of the Virgin Mary with arms outstretched which bears the inscription, "Par Marie à Jésus" (Through Mary to Jesus).

Completing this Byzantine style church is a dome, and on the outside the dome is capped by a gilt crown and cross which were gifts from the people of Ireland in 1924.

UNDERGROUND BASILICA OF ST PIUS X

Because of the large crowds expected to descend on Lourdes for the centenary of the apparitions, this underground weather-proof Basilica was built in 1958,and was consecrated by the man who later that year would become Pope John XXIII.

Its starkness is in complete contrast to the other earlier places of worship. Designed by the architect Pierre Vago, it is one of the largest buildings of the world, being oval-shaped with a length of about 220 yards (c.200 metres) and a width of about 90 yards (c.85 metres). Its ceiling is low at about 33 feet (c.10 metres) and there are 58 pre-stressed concrete pillars which support the structure, creating 29 porticoes which offer maximum visibility of the raised sanctuary area and altar in the middle. In the height of the season this building has to be prepared for in excess of 20,000 worshippers.

The Blessed Sacrament is reserved in the Pax Christi Chapel as are some relics of Pope St Pius X. To the left of the bishop's chair is a chapel of St Thérèse of Lisieux and the red mosaics were the gift of English pilgrims in 1974.

A fine organ supports the singing of the assembly at the two International Masses held here each week. The walls of the ramps are decorated with Stations of the Cross by Denys de Solère, and a Gemmail (back-lit stained glass) series of the Rosary by Robert Falcucci. At the bottom are scenes of the apparitions of Our Lady to Bernadette. All three of these are accessible to wheelchairs.

CHURCH OF SAINT BERNADETTE

Blessed in 1988, this church faces the Grotto on the opposite side of the river. It is built on the spot in the meadow where Bernadette stood for the last time to see the Virgin Mary.

The church can accommodate more than one pilgrimage at a time by means of huge sliding partitions which allow for a multi-purpose use. Continuing the starkness of the Underground Basilica, St Bernadette's is devoid of the rich decoration of the older churches, even to the point of being designed with heating and air-conditioning pipes as part of the atmosphere.

It can hold about 5,000 seated pilgrims and 350 wheelchairs. It has a sacristy, eight conference rooms, toilets and a first aid post. Connected by a covered walkway is the Hemicycle which is an amphitheatre-shaped lecture-room, and this also doubles to accommodate 500 for worship. In this building there are four more conference rooms for small groups.

ADORATION CHAPEL

Blessed in 1995, the Adoration Chapel is found by taking a path which leads behind St Bernadette's Church to the left and adjacent to the meadow.

As the normal place of exposition of the reserved sacrament, the building is built to symbolize the Tent of Meeting (Exodus 40:16-21) where God lived with the Hebrew people during their travels in the desert. Shaped like a tent, its focal point is the tabernacle made from gilded wood which is carved into a column of fire, yet another biblical reference to God's presence in the luminous cloud (Exodus 40:34-38). Twelve columns around the building symbolize Christ's abiding presence in the Church, the New Jerusalem, built on the twelve foundations bearing the names of the apostles and the Lamb (Revelation 21:9-14).

There is an upper section or balcony intended for those who wish to stay for longer periods of prayer. Pilgrims are asked to avoid anything which would be likely to distract others from prayer and recollection, and to keep the silence at all times.

RECONCILIATION CHAPEL

Penance is at the heart of the message of Lourdes, and plentiful provision is made for the sacrament of Reconciliation. The new Reconciliation Chapel is now more central than its predecessor and can be found at the edge of Rosary Square to the right of the Crowned Statue as you face the Basilica. Priests from all over the world are available for confessions in all the major European languages.

ST JOSEPH'S CHAPEL

This is a small underground building which is situated off the Esplanade, close to the Abri St Michel. Not immediately visible from the Esplanade, it is approached down a path which also leads to toilets. It has facilities for about 450 sick pilgrims and staff from the Acceuil, which is the long building immediately behind it, to worship there. At other times it is used for pilgrimage liturgies by medium-sized groups.

STATIONS OF THE CROSS

A high set of Stations, inaugurated in 1912, starts next to the Reconciliation Chapel and is not suitable for those who have difficulty getting about. Shortly after the entrance is a memorial to the "Pilgrimage of Sorrow", 33 French pilgrims who died in a train accident in 1922. At the first Station is a

Scala Sancta, a Holy Stairs, similar to that in Rome which purports to come from the house of Pontius Pilate in Jerusalem. Some pilgrims mount these stairs on their knees as a sign of penance.

The 15 Stations, with figures in cast iron overlaid with bronze, follow a track up the Espélugues mountain for about a mile (c.1,600 metres) to the Calvary. At the top is the Espélugues cave where prehistoric remains have been found.

A low set of Stations for people in wheelchairs and those with difficulty in walking may be found on the right bank of the River Gave, close to the bridge and on the flat. Almost opposite is a statue of St Margaret of Scotland, a gift of the Scottish people in 1929.

The low Stations are marked in coloured lines on the concrete. Unlike the traditional Way of the Cross they have two extra Stations. A 15th Station announces, "With certain hope and complete faith, the Virgin awaits the Third Day" and a 16th Station proclaims, "He has risen as he said. Alleluia."

PARISH CHURCH

Situated off the Rue St Pierre in the old town, the present church is not that which Bernadette knew, since the original parish church was destroyed by fire in 1905. Construction of the new church had begun as long ago as 1875. It contains a number of reminders of Bernadette's time including the baptismal font in which she was baptized in 1844, a statue of Madonna and Child, and the confessional of Abbé Peyramale who was parish priest at the time of the apparitions. In the crypt below is his tomb and white marble monument.

THE OLD PRESBYTERY

The place still stands at 7,Chaussée Maransin where Bernadette delivered the messages to the priests from Our Lady. The austere-looking building is now a public lending library.

POOR CLARES CONVENT

Just over the Pont Vieux, on the left when climbing up the Rue de la Grotte, is the Convent of the Poor Clares (Les Clarisses). For shoppers and hotel residents in this part of town it offers an opportunity for quiet prayer without having to make the longer trip down into the Sanctuary areas.

BERNADETTE'S BIRTHPLACE (THE BOLY MILL)

Almost hidden by a narrow and twisting road, the Boly Mill (Moulin Boly), on Rue Bernadette Soubirous, is named after an English doctor who lived there during the XVII century. It was the birthplace of Bernadette and her home for most of her childhood years.

The ground floor consists of the kitchen which doubled as a communal living room, and the mill itself where her father worked by using the water from the Lapacca stream.

Upstairs, (although if approached from one side this can at first appear to be the ground level) is the room in which Bernadette was born, and a second mill room.

The rooms have articles which recreate the scene as it would have been during the Soubirous family's time.

LE CACHOT

Rather like the Boly Mill, this small place can easily be missed or passed by. It is the tiny disused prison at 15, Rue des Petits-Fossés, where Bernadette and her family were forced to live after they were evicted from the Boly Mill.

The cold, unwelcoming cell with its stone sink and small fireplace contains souvenirs of the family including one of Bernadette's socks and a pair of clogs. There are also some photographs dating from that time and a statue of Our Lady which used to be in the old Parish Church. It is possible for a very small group of people to celebrate Mass here.

THE HOSPICE

This is the place which included a hospital and school run by the Sisters of Nevers, on Rue Alexandre Marqui, where Bernadette prepared for her First Communion and where she eventually lodged with the sisters before leaving to become a nun.

On view is the Oratory where Bernadette made her First Communion and the Old Parlour where there are several souvenirs of her time there.

THE SOUBIROUS TOMB

Although Bernadette's body lies in the chapel of the Sisters of Nevers at their Motherhouse, her parents and family were buried in Lourdes.

The Égalité Cemetery houses the family tomb. Once inside the cemetery gates take the path to the right. The next path to the left leads down to a war memorial and a iron cross. Next to these is the Soubirous family vault, clearly visible by its polished stone of grey granite.

The cemetery itself is best approached over the Pont Vieux and up the Rue de la Grotte, looking eventually for signs marked "Égalité".

Entrances

1 St Michael's Gate
2 St Joseph's Gate
3 Upper Basilica Entrance
4 Lacets Gate
5 Meadow Entrance
6 Boissarie Entrance

7 Grotto
8 Water taps
9 Baths
10 Crowned Virgin
11 Information Centre
12 Pastoral Information Centre
13 Permanences
14 Lost Property
15 Picnic
16 Meeting/Conference Rooms

17 Hémicycle Mont-Carmel
18 Salle Notre-Dame
19 Salle Mgr Laurence
20 Salle Mgr Theas
21 Les Rotondes

Churches

22 Upper Basilica
23 Crypt
24 Rosary Basilica
25 Esplanade Chapel
26 Underground Basilica
27 St Bernadette's Church
28 St Joseph's Chapel
29 Chapel of Reconciliation

30 Way of the Cross
31 Way of the Cross (level ground)

32 Musée Tresor
33 Accueil Notre-Dame
34 Accueil St-Frai
35 Hospitality Offices
36 Medical Bureau
37 Meeting Pavilions
38 Museum
39 Bookshop
40 Cinéma Bernadette
41 Office Cité St-Pierre
42 Pilgrims' Shelter

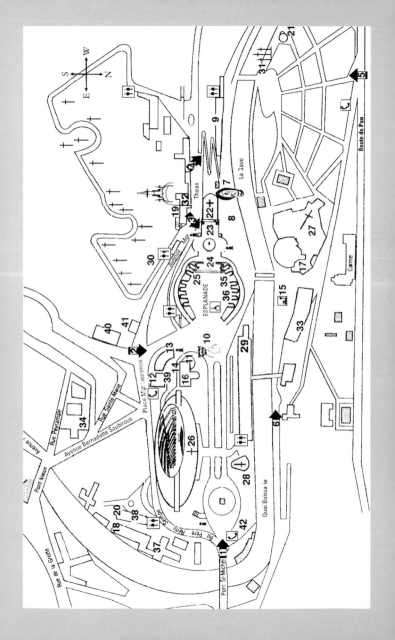

SEASONAL PILGRIMAGE TIMETABLES

In addition to the specific arrangements and activities made by national and diocesan pilgrimages, there are a number of public events which are celebrated communally each day.

These activities are scaled down when the pilgrimage season has finished, and so there are two timetables in operation: one from Easter until All Saints (November 1st), and another from All Saints until Easter. Both timetables are given below, but changes can take place and so it is always advisable to check the on the pilgrimage events each day. They are posted around 6pm the previous day outside the Forum Information building.

FROM EASTER UNTIL NOVEMBER 1ST

Masses:
International Mass every Sunday and Wednesday at 9.30am in the Underground Basilica of Pius X

International Youth Mass in St Bernadette's Church every Thursday night at 8.30pm during July, and every Saturday night at 8.30pm during August.

In various languages at the Grotto each day, the last mass beginning at 9.45am

English Mass every day at 9am in the Chapel of St Cosmas and St Damian situated in the Acceuil Jean-Paul II (former Acceuil Notre Dame)

Adoration:
Exposition daily in Tent of Adoration from 8.30am to 5pm The Adoration Chapel is open for Adoration from 6pm to midnight.

Confessions:
Confessions in English are heard in the Reconciliation Chapel from 10am to 11.15am and from 2.30pm to 6.00pm

Processions:
Procession of the Blessed Sacrament and Blessing of the Sick daily at 5pm beginning from the Adoration Chapel, near St Bernadette's Church. It proceeds to the St Pius X Underground Basilica where Eucharistic Adoration and the Blessing of the Sick take place. Only exceptionally is it held in the open on Rosary Square

Marian Celebration and Torchlight Procession each night at 9pm beginning in the Grotto

Baths:
Open on weekdays from 9am to 11am and 2.30pm to 4pm and on Sundays from 2pm until 4pm

FROM NOVEMBER UNTIL MARCH

Masses:
Mass in English daily at 9am in St Michael's Chapel, to the right of the entrance to the Crypt

Adoration:
Monday to Friday from 12noon to 3pm in the Crypt Sunday from 11am to 3pm

Confessions:
In the Reconciliation Chapel from 10am to 11am and from 2.30pm to 3.30pm

Baths:
Weekdays from 10am to 11am and from 2.30pm to 3.30pm Sundays and Feastdays from 2.30pm to 4pm

ONE DAY PILGRIMS

If you are visiting for just one day and wish to make the most of pilgrimage opportunities while in Lourdes, there is a special programme offered for Day Pilgrims from 1st July until 30th September.

You will be accompanied by priests and seminarians who lead day pilgrimages according to different language groups. There is no need to book in advance, just present yourself at the statue of the Crowned Virgin at 9am and/or 2.15pm. Similar activities are available for children and for young people at the same place and time.

The daily timetable and programme may differ, but the One Day Pilgrimage usually includes:

• Celebration of Mass

• Way of the Cross

• Guided tour in the footsteps of Bernadette

• Blessed Sacrament Procession

• Torchlight Procession

Opportunity for the Sacrament of Reconciliation is usually given, and pilgrims may also wish to seek some form of spiritual direction.

In case this programme may need to be altered for some reason, always check beforehand on the notice boards at the Forum Information for starting times.

SOME USEFUL WORDS AND PHRASES

Many people who work in the hotels, cafes and shops of Lourdes also speak or understand English, so it is unlikely that you will be stranded with no way of making yourself understood. For the ambitious traveller a French phrase-book may prove useful. For those who just want to recognize signs and find their way around, a very basic list of routine words is given below. For those who speak a little French, then a few words of politeness in a shop or hotel is a sign of goodwill.

AROUND THE DOMAINE

L'Église	Church
La Chapelle	Chapel
La Grotte	Grotto
Les Piscines	Baths
Porte St Joseph/Michel	St Joseph's/Michael's Gate
Les Permanences	Pilgrimage Offices
Chemin de la Croix	Stations of the Cross
La Prairie	Meadow
Poste de Secours	First Aid Point

PILGRIMAGE WORDS

La Messe	Mass
Le Chapelet	Rosary
Le Missel	Missal
La Cierge	Candle
Les Offrandes	Offerings
Les Pèlerins	Pilgrims
Le Pèlerinage	Pilgrimage

IN THE HOTEL

Rez-de-chaussée	Ground floor
1er étage, 2ème étage	1st floor, 2nd floor
Ascenseur	Lift (elevator)
La Clé	Key
La Chambre numéro 99	Room 99
Sortie	Exit
Sortie de secours	Emergency exit
L'Addition	Bill
Le Petit Déjeuner	Breakfast
Le Déjeuner	Lunch
Le Dîner	Dinner (Supper)

OUT AND ABOUT

Librairie	Bookshop
Pharmacie	Chemist's shop
Boulangerie	Baker's shop
Boucherie	Butcher's shop
Épicerie	Grocer's shop
Confisserie	Confectioner's shop (sweets/candy)
Tabac	Tobacconist's shop
Supermarché	Supermarket
La Gare (SNCF)	Railway Station
Arrêt d'autobus	Bus-stop
Office de Tourisme	Tourist Office

TIMES OF THE DAY

Bonjour	Good morning
Bon après-midi	Good afternoon
Bonsoir	Good evening
Bon nuit	Good night
Aujourd'hui	Today
Hier	Yesterday
Hier soir	Last night
Demain	Tomorrow
Demain matin	Tomorrow morning
Au revoir	Goodbye
Adieu	Farewell

IN THE CAFE

Oui, s'il vous plaît	Yes, please
Merci	Thank you
Non, merci	No, thank you
Un verre de/une tasse de	A glass of/a cup of...
L'Eau (minerale)	Water (mineral)
Vin (rouge/blanc)	Wine (red/white)
Bière	Beer
Lait	Milk
Un café (au lait)	A (white) coffee
Deux thés	2 teas
Trois citronades	3 lemonades
Quatre croques monsieurs	4 toasted sandwiches (ham + cheese)
Cinq gâteaux	5 cakes
(Plus) grand	Large (larger)
(Plus) petit	Small (smaller)

Froid	Cold
(Très) chaud	(Very) Hot
Blanc	White
Noir	Black
Ça coute combien?	How much is that?
(Trop) cher	(Too) Dear
Bonne marché	Cheap

WHERE AND WHEN

C'est la route juste pour..?	Is this the right way to…?
À quelle heure…?	At what time…?
Où est…?	Where is…?
C'est loin d'ici…?	Is it far from here…?
C'est près d'ici…?	Is it near here…?
À la droite…	On the right
À la gauche…	On the left
Tout droite…	Straight on
Au coin de la rue…	At the corner of the street

VISITING THE LOCAL AREA

THE OLD TOWN

Many pilgrims to Lourdes become so preoccupied with the central pilgrimage area that they never venture out of the hotels and shops district, and consequently miss out on a completely different side to Lourdes: the old town. In fact, it is sometimes said that Lourdes is two towns, or at least a town with two faces.

Why not spend a few hours looking round the upper town? Here you will see a provincial town as pretty as any other, with its variety of shops, its colourful set of street-traders, its halles (covered market), as well as a whole series of good restaurants and hotels.

The old town has its own proud civic history, displayed in its monuments and buildings of architectural interest. A casual walk along the main street from the hospital end (Chaussée Maransin) to the Mairie end (Ave. Maréchal Foch) will reveal all the signs of daily living: schools, hospital, shops, supermarket, Post Office, swimming pool, market etc, as well as the more august signs of a thriving community: chateau, monuments and statues, the Palais des Congrès, Forum, Mairie, and several picturesque squares. Any short detour from this main road is rewarded by little twisting streets which boast their own beauty and history.

For those wishing to know more about the background to the old town, there is an Association called "Amis du Vieux Lourdes" which runs walking tours each morning and afternoon. Each tour lasts about 75 minutes. So if you would like to see some of the sites which escape the average tourist, including the "rediscovered" Moulin Baudéan, where Bernadette's family lived in 1863 and 1864, then ask about the "Lourdes Découverte" tours. They usually leave from opposite the Red Cross office at 54, Rue du Bourg, but for times and further details enquire at the Tourist Office.

BARTRÈS

Bartrès is less than three miles away from Lourdes and is accessible either on foot, via the Avenue Célestin-Romain, or by the bus which leaves from St Joseph's Gate.

Bernadette stayed at Bartrès for two periods in her life. The first was when she went for 18 months as an infant to be nursed by her foster-mother Marie Aravant-Lagüe. Later, in 1857, she returned there to work on the farm as a shepherdess.

Points of interest include:

- The Bourg farmhouse: this has been restored after fire and which contains furniture and implements which would have been familiar to Bernadette.

- The Bergerie (Shepherd's Hut): this is the sheepfold where Bernadette looked after the sheep. It is located up a stony hill path and is not accessible to most handicapped people.

- The Parish Church of St John the Baptist (Église Paroissiale): inside there are gilt carvings dating from the XVII century and outside there is a small churchyard which contains the grave of Marie Aravant-Lagüe who nursed Bernadette.

BÉTHARRAM

Bétharram is about 10 miles outside Lourdes on the road to Pau, passing through St Pé de Bigorre. From the XV century there has been a shrine at Bétharram to Our Lady.

It was also here that Bernadette met Michael Garricoits, the founder of the Congregation of Priests of the Sacred Heart.

Today it attracts many tourists to see its underground caves which are on five different labyrinthine floors. They are superimposed on top of each other as nature over the years has created one level after another.

Details on bus excursions to Bétharram are available in most hotels or from couriers and travel agents.

LAC DE LOURDES

The Lourdes Lake has no connection with the religious events which took place at Lourdes, but is a popular venue in the pilgrimage season for those who want to take advantage of the refreshing water in the summer heat. You can practise your swimming or take part in various aquatic sports.

Situated on the outskirts of Lourdes, off the N640 Pau road, it is often a place that can be visited in conjunction with an excursion to Bartrès.

PIC DU JER

The summit of the Pic Du Jer is visible in the distance from many parts of Lourdes and a regular local service bus leaves from the centre of the old town.

There is a funicular railway that takes visitors to the top of the mountain which stands at 1000 metres and from which there are panoramic views of Lourdes and of the surrounding Pyrénées range. It is a popular site especially for picnics.

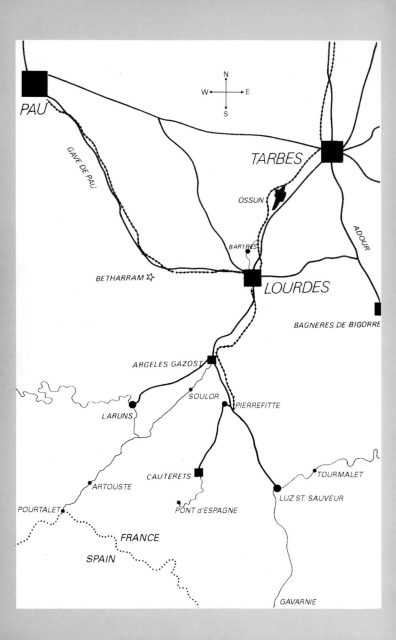

TOURING THE PYRÉNÉES

Lourdes makes a perfect base for touring the Pyrénées on half-day or full-day excursions. It is within easy reach of a number of mountain resorts which offer overnight accommodation, and is an excellent place to break a road journey through Europe en route to Spain or Portugal, taking in the southern French resorts of Bayonne, Biarritz or St Jean de Luz, before crossing into the Basque region of Spain to Irun, San Sebastian, and further afield. If you decide to cross into Spain, regardless of what might be the current regulations relating to travel documentation, it is always advisable to take your passport with you.

Below are just a few of the options available in the Pyrénées area. Approximate round-trip distances from Lourdes are given in brackets, and suggested outline routes are offered, although a good road map is of course necessary. For this reason no road numbers have been given in the route details, to discourage anyone from relying solely on this book. For those without their own transport, tourist buses visit most of these places, and details of prices, timetables and destinations are available in most of the hotels, or from couriers and travel agents.

HALF-DAY TRIPS

Les Grottes de Médous (50km/30m)
A pleasant half-day jaunt to see the famous underground caves, rather like those of Bétharram, but generally acknowledged to be the finest in the Pyrénées. Take the boat ride underground. On the way back a visit to the Spa (station thermale) at Bagnères-de-Bigorre is recommended.

Outline Route:
About 25km outside Lourdes on the Bagnères-de-Bigorre road.

Pau (80km/50m)

A choice of roads will take you to Pau, but if you take the St Pé de Bigorre route then you can pay a quick visit to the Sanctuary at Bétharram. To visit Bétharram underground caves and Pau requires a full day. Once in Pau be sure to see the old city and especially the Castle of Henry IV.

Outline Route:

From Lourdes on the Pau road via St Pé de Bigorre. On the return journey travel back via Soumoulou and Pontacq.

Gavarnie (100km/60m)

About 20,000 years ago a glacier scooped out the landscape between Gavarnie and Lourdes, tearing out vast stretches of limestone rock to form the deep gorges and valleys with their corresponding peaks. This is known as the Gavarnie Cirque. It affords spectacular views of peaks and waterfalls, of wildlife and rustic domesticity. In the town of Gavarnie (at 1,360 metres), you can take a ride on a mule to the base of the Cirque, do some shopping, or just have a meal. There is also an interesting XIV century church.

Outline Route:

Go through the Argelès valley, Pierrefitte, the Luz gorge and Luz St Sauveur, and through Gedre following signs for Gavarnie.

Pont d'Espagne (80km/50m)

As its name suggests, this trip goes to the end of the road that bridges France and Spain, although it peters out at a height of 1,500 metres a few miles before reaching the border. The first part of the route is the same as that for the Gavarnie trip, and it branches off at Pierrefitte. At Pont d'Espagne think of visiting Lake Gaube either on foot or by chairlift (télésiège). A stop at the Spa of Cauterets is worthwhile and the view of the waterfalls from La Raillère is memorable. In season skiing is available at Caillan.

Outline Route:

Go through the Argelès valley as with the Gavarnie itinerary but turn off the Gavarnie road at Pierrefitte, passing through Cauterets and following signs for Pont d'Espagne.

Col du Soulor and Lac d'Estaing (100km/60m)

A favourite trip of many of the local Lourdes people, this journey takes us up into the mountain pass of Soulor (at 1,445 metres) and to the Lake of Estaing. Breath-taking scenery and fresh mountain air can be a pleasant change from the sultry summer heat.

Outline Route:

Take the road towards Bétharram, then follow signs through Callibel and Ferrière to Col du Soulor. On the way back continue the loop by descending through the twisting pass towards Arrens-Marsous, and thence to Argelès-Gazost and Lourdes.

Col du Tourmalet (100km/60m)

The Tourmalet Pass stands at 2,114 metres and affords some of the most magnificent views in the whole of the Pyrénées. It is another trip for those who prefer the mountain freshness to the city heat. On the way down visit La Mongie, take a look at the skiing facilities of the area, the Ardour avec Gripp valley, and Ste Marie-de-Campan. The Spa of Bagnères-de-Bigorre is worth a visit.

Outline Route:

Take the Argelès road and go through Pierrefitte and Luz, then follow signs for Barèges which take you up to the Pass. On the way back continue the loop by going through La Mongie following the signs for Bagnères-de Bigorre, and turn off the Tarbes road for Lourdes just after Trebons.

Col du Pourtalet (160km/100m)

For those wishing to set foot on Spanish soil, the Col du Pourtalet trip offers the opportunity of the usual mountain experience, including the Pic du Midi d'Ossau at 2,885 metres, with just a hint of a new culture over the border. The Pourtalet Pass stands at 1.802 metres. The closest Spanish villages are at Lanueza and Sallent de Gallego.

Outline Route:

Go in the direction of Bétharram. A short distance after Bétharram follow signs for Asson and Louvie-Juzon. Continue along this road through the Ossau valley in the direction of Laruns and pass through Gabas towards the Pass and the border.

FULL-DAY TRIPS

Combination Gavarnie and Pont d'Espagne (140km/85m)

This trip allows a whole day to combine the two half-day trips to Gavarnie and Pont d'Espagne described above. On the way there, it worth taking a look at Luz and at the famous bridge of Napoleon III.

Outline Route:

The best way to combine the two trips is to follow the directions given above to Gavarnie and then to return along the road to Pierrefitte and follow the directions given above for Pont d'Espagne.

Lac d'Artouste and Col du Pourtalet (180km/115m)

This beautiful journey takes us into the mountains and the "pays des isards," into rocky crags and rhododendrons, walking country favoured by hikers. A cable-car rises to 2,000 metres and the peak of Sagette. The miniature narrow-gauge railway affords panoramic views on its 10km (6m) journey up to the Artouste lake (1,964 metres), and the specially created Spanish Aragon-style village of Fabrèges caters both for the day visitor and those wishing to spend a few days there, with hotels, camp sites and restaurants.

Outline Route:

Follow the same itinerary as if travelling to Col Du Pourtalet via Bétharram, Louvie-Juzon, the Ossau valley and Laruns. Before reaching Col du Pourtalet there will be signs to Artouste. On the way back take in Col du Pourtalet and return by the same route.

Panoramic National Park and Lakes Drive (240km/150m)

This is a full day's journey through panoramic countryside and mountain passes, into the isolated lake regions, returning via the relatively populated area around Tarbes.

Outline Route:

Follow the road from Lourdes in the following directions, stopping whenever it seems suitable: To Bagnères-de-Bigorre, and then to Col d'Aspin (1,489 metres). Through the pass towards Arreau, the Aure valley and the ski station of Saint-Lary. After Fabian take the road up to the lake region of Oredon, Aumar, Aubert and rising to the Cap-de-Long Dam at 2.160 metres, itself at the foot of the towering Neovielle (3,090 metres). On the way back return via the Neste valley, taking the road to Saint-Lary and Arreau. Then instead of retracing your steps, continue along this route towards Lannemezan and follow the road through the more populous regions of Tournay and Tarbes before arriving back in Lourdes.

Biarritz (320km/200m)

Biarritz is one of the most popular of the Basque resorts in France, and is able to be visited from Lourdes in a day, provided that a reasonably early start is made. Twelve hours from start to finish should allow for a good six hours in Biarritz. The route is straightforward and the motorway roads are fast. Once in Biarritz you may care to take advantage of the famous beaches, spend time shopping or sampling the food in the many fish restaurants, visiting the Rock of the Virgin (Rocher de la Vierge) or the Marine Museum (Musée de la Mer).

Outline Route:

From Lourdes follow the Pau signs and pick up the motorway (autoroute) in the direction of Bayonne, travelling through Orthez, Peyrehorade, and Bayonne. Return by the same route.

THE PILGRIM'S A-Z OF LOURDES

An easy-to-use, quick guide to people, places and services for the visitor to Lourdes.

ABRI ST MICHEL

This is a hostel, situated just on the right after entering the Domaine by St Michael's Gate. It is used as a place to lodge by brancardiers since it can be more flexible than an ordinary hotel to the hours worked by brancardiers, and also offers a more affordable accommodation.

ACCUEILS

An accueil means a reception place or accommodation building. In Lourdes there are several of these. Some exist to give information and to take bookings for various events, like the Permanences (Pilgrimage Offices) on the right of the path going down from St Joseph's gate towards the Square. Other accueils afford nursing accommodation for sick pilgrims. Until recently this accommodation was offered at the Accueil Notre Dame, the Accueil Marie Saint Frai (formerly called Notre Dame des Douleurs) and the Accueil Sainte Bernadette, but the building of the new 904 bed Accueil Notre-Dame in 1997 on the opposite side of the Gave has permitted a wider and more up-to-date provision for the sick. Its former site now houses the Acceuil Jean-Paul II which includes a first aid post, the Medical Bureau, meeting rooms and chapels, and a hospitality section. In addition, the rebuilt Accueil Marie Saint-Frai was completed in 1998.

BARTRÈS

Bartrès is the small village, a couple of miles north of Lourdes, where Bernadette went as a small baby to be wet-nursed, and to which she returned for a while as a shepherdess shortly before the apparitions took place. For further information see p.60.

BASILICAS

Upper Basilica:

This church, also known as the Basilica of the Immaculate Conception, is situated at the top of the complex of buildings in Rosary Square, built over the Crypt which itself stands above the Rosary Basilica. It was consecrated in 1876. For more details see p.43.

Rosary Basilica:

The Rosary Basilica is the church which is (almost) on ground level and overlooks the Esplanade with the Square extending from a flight of broad steps, which give access to the Basilica's main doors. It was opened in 1889. For more details see p.43.

St Pius X Basilica (Underground Basilica):

Consecrated in 1958, this is the cavernous Basilica used for very large gatherings, particularly the International Mass on Wednesdays and Sundays. The main entrances are from ramps which descend between the Permanences buildings and the Forum Information Centre, on the right when facing the Statue of the Crowned Virgin, and also from paths off the Esplanade at the St Michael's Gate end. For more details see p.44.

BATHS

The Baths (Piscines) are situated in the Domaine area, facing the river and just along from the Grotto. For more details see p.42.

BEGGARS

Please do not give any money to the beggars no matter how plausible they appear. A system has been devised to help those in genuine need. It is called Entraide St Martin and is in the Secours Catholique building outside St Joseph's Gate. People in real need may be referred here.

BÉTHARRAM

Situated a short drive from Lourdes, Bétharram is famous for its numerous caves and for being a shrine to the Blessed Virgin Mary. For more details see p.60.

BLESSED SACRAMENT PROCESSION

This takes place daily at 5pm and is followed by the Blessing of the Sick in Rosary Square. For more details and an outline of the Service see p.151.

BOLY MILL

This is the place (Moulin de Boly) in Lourdes where Bernadette was born and where her family lived for a period while their father, François, was employed there as a miller. For more details see p.48.

BOOKSHOP

On the ground floor of the Pastoral Affairs Centre (Centre d'Animation Pastorale), on the path leading to the Underground Basilica and behind the Forum Information building, is the Bookshop (Librairie) which sells English language religious books, records, cassettes, copies of the music used in Lourdes, postcards, phonecards and the Lourdes Magazine. It is open from 8am to 12 noon and from 1.30pm to 6pm every day except Sunday when it is open from 9am to 12 noon.

BRANCARDIERS

The word means "stretcher-bearers", but is used to designate men who care for the sick by lifting people, pushing wheelchairs and carriages, and marshalling at public events. More permanent brancardiers based in Lourdes wear leather straps from their shoulders, whereas most temporary brancardiers travelling with a pilgrimage wear canvas straps. These straps or braces are now seen as symbols of what once were used to lift the stretchers.

BUSES

There is a useful bus which leaves every fifteen minutes from St Joseph's gate and travels through most of the central streets of Lourdes towards the railway station (signposted either La Gare or SNCF). En route it goes through the old town of Lourdes where pilgrims will find the parish church, market halls, shops, Post Office, Tourist Office etc. Other buses leave from the same place and go in the direction of Esplanade du Paradis and Avenue Peyramale. For those wishing to explore the Pic du Jer, there is a bus which leaves regularly from the old town centre.

CACHOT

The Cachot is the little prison in which Bernadette and her family lived when her father was out of work and they fell upon hard times. For more details see p.48.

CAMPING

There are a about 20 camp sites around Lourdes, and in the wider Pyrénées area there are numerous places where camping is available. In the summertime camping is particularly popular with families and young people's groups, many of whom combine a camping holiday with their pilgrimage. Information on sites, prices and facilities may be obtained from the Tourist Office: Office Municipal de Tourisme, Place Peyramale (in the old town). Tel. 05.62.42.77.40. For the Young People's Camp telephone 05.62.42.79.95.

CANDLES

Candles are available in the shops, along with paper candle-holders containing the words to prayers and hymns used in the Torchlight Procession. Candles to be left in the votive stands are purchased on a self-service basis from stands below the right ramp of the Rosary Basilica on the Grotto side. Prices are nominal and are clearly marked. Very large candles, suitable for dioceses or organizations, may be purchased from the Mass Bureau to the left of the Basilica.

CASTLE

The castle (Château Fort) dominates the town of Lourdes and a fortified building has stood there since Roman times. For periods in the thirteenth and fourteenth century it was under the control of the English crown, and Lord Elgin was imprisoned there in 1803 by Napoleon. Today it houses a museum of Pyrenean art and culture. Some of the fittings which were in the parish church at the time of Bernadette are now to be found on display in the castle. Panoramic views are to be had from the top of the building. It is open from 9.00 to 11.00am and from 2.00 to 6.00pm. Steps lead up to it from Place du Fort, and the Rampe du Fort returns the visitor to ground level. There is also a lift.

CEMETERIES

The original cemetery, in which the Soubirous family's tomb can be seen, is the Cimetière de l' Égalité. Follow the signs marked "Égalité" from the Rue de la Grotte. Behind the parish church on the Rue de Langelle, there is a second cemetery with national vaults in which are buried the bodies of pilgrims who came to Lourdes and died whilst on pilgrimage. Recently a third cemetery, dedicated to the Good Shepherd (Bon Pasteur), has been opened a little way outside the town, on the road which leads to the lake (Lac de Lourdes).

CHANGING MONEY

You can buy euros in Post Offices, at the station and airport and often in your hotel, besides the usual Bureaux de Change and banks. When changing foreign currency at a commercial outlet, it is worth checking whether a commission is to be charged or not. An advantage with buying euros before leaving home is that, if you keep the receipt from your transaction, many travel businesses will not charge you for reconverting the euros when you get home. You may also find that for larger transactions your hotel and some of the shops will accept any major currency.

CHAPELS

Adoration Chapel:

This new chapel is situated at the left side of St Bernadette's Church, approached from a path that leads round the back of the church on the meadow side. It is reserved exclusively for Exposition and therefore for quiet, personal prayer. For more details see p.45.

Hospitality Chapel:

The Hospitality Chapel is to be found at the entrance of the Rosary Basilica, just inside on the left hand side. It stands among the fifteen small chapels which recount the mysteries of the Rosary.

Pax Christi Chapel:

The Pax Christi Chapel is the place of reservation of the Blessed Sacrament, situated in the Underground Basilica of St Pius X.

Reconciliation Chapel:

This chapel, to the right of the Crowned Statue at the edge of Rosary Square, is reserved solely for the celebration of the sacrament of Reconciliation. For further details see Confessions p.75

St Bernadette's Chapel:

In the corner of Rosary Square, underneath the left hand ramp, there is an open-air worship area with an altar underneath a canopy. It is known as St Bernadette's Chapel or the Esplanade Altar.

St Joseph's Chapel:

A small underground chapel seating 450 people, situated about two thirds way along the Esplanade, just past the old Acceuil Notre Dame. For more details see p.46.

CHAPLAINS

Many of the chaplains who lead diocesan pilgrimages stay at the Chaplains' Residence, close to the Reconciliation Chapel on Avenue Mgr Théas. Tel.05.62.42.78.78. Fax. 05.62.42.79.38

CHILDREN

A number of activities are on offer for children who speak French, including:

- Children's Pilgrimage: meet during July and August at 9am and 2.30pm at the statue of the Crowned Virgin
- Blessing of children: daily in July and August at 3.30pm on the podium next to St Bernadette's Church

CHOIRS

Choirs and individual singers who wish to participate in the International Masses and the daily Blessed Sacrament and Torchlight Processions are invited to do so. Please arrive an hour before the service.

CHURCHES

Parish Church:

The Parish Church (Église Paroissiale), was begun to be built in 1875 and therefore is not the one Bernadette knew as a girl. It is to be found in the old town. For more details see p.47.

St Bernadette's Church:

Built opposite the Grotto on the other side of the river, it was blessed in 1988. For more details see p.45 . See also Basilicas, Chapels.

CINEMAS

Two cinemas show films, sometimes dubbed into English or with English subtitles, which deal with the events and the phenomena of Lourdes. They are:

Cinema Bernadette:
This is near St Joseph's Gate on the Rue Mgr Schoepfer

Cinema de la Forêt:
This is situated near the river, beyond the baths and the statue of St Margaret

For all of these, consult the boards for times of daily showings.

CITÉ ST PIERRE

In 1956 the Cité Secours St Pierre, often known as the City of the Poor, was opened to accommodate up to six hundred people who wish to visit Lourdes on pilgrimage but who would find it financially impossible to stay in the usual hotels. These often include refugees, poor people and those from countries which are economically disadvantaged. Provision for these guests depends upon the generosity of those who are financially more fortunate. The twenty minute walk from the Domaine is not recommended for those who have difficulty in getting about, but there is a bus which goes to the Cité Secours St Pierre from the Secours Catholique office opposite St Joseph's Gate. Upon arrival visitors may take a one hour guided tour.

CONFESSIONS

Most pilgrimages offer the opportunity to celebrate communally the sacrament of reconciliation whilst in Lourdes. If you wish, however, there is a special place set aside for hearing confessions in the six langauges of the Sanctuary. The Chapel of Reconciliation (Chapelle des

Confessions) is situated in the Domaine to the right of the Crowned Statue. From April to October confessions are heard from 10am to 11.15am and from 2.30pm to 6pm. From November to March they are heard from 10am to 11am and from 2.30pm to 3.30pm.but it is advisable to double-check these times.

CROWNED STATUE

The statue of the Crowned Virgin (La Vierge Couronnée) stands at the edge of Rosary Square and is a favourite meeting point for pilgrims. For fuller details see p.41.

CRYPT

The Crypt is underneath the Upper Basilica. It was dedicated on Pentecost 1866, the day that official pilgrimages to Lourdes started. For more details see p.42.

DAY PILGRIMS

A special service of a guided tour and spiritual exercises is provided for those who will only be in Lourdes for one day. For full details of what is offered see p.54.

DIALYSIS

Patients who require dialysis may use the St John the Baptist Dialysis Centre, opened in 1986. It is found on Route de Bartrès, Tel. 05.62.94.26.25. Requests need to be made in advance of the pilgrimage and through one of the doctors officially assigned to the pilgrimage.

DIORAMA

The story of Lourdes may be seen in a series of tableaux at the Diorama, just to the right of the Cinema Bernadette on Rue Mgr Schoepfer, opposite St Joseph's Gate. There is no charge but offerings may be made.

DOMAINE

Domaine is the word used to describe the large enclosed park-like area in which are housed the principal sites which together form the Shrine of Our Lady of Lourdes. Sometimes called the Domaine of Massabielle or Domaine de la Grotte, it is the central area where public worship takes place. Daytime access to the Domaine is via a series of gates which enclose the area open from 5.00am until midnight. From midnight until 5.00am the only means of entering the Domaine is via the Lacets Gate. Silence is requested at all times in the Domaine.

DRINKS

Water in the hotels is drinkable but many pilgrims either use bottled water or a flask of the Lourdes water which can be obtained from the taps at the Grotto. Like most French towns, Lourdes boasts a wide selection of wines, and the hotels are pleased to recommend some fine vintages which are produced locally. Beer is usually of the continental lager type. It is served in various sizes: petite, grande, distinguée and formidable. The latter is usually more than most people would wish to consume. A shandy is a bière panachée

Freshly-squeezed fruit drinks (eg citron pressé) are popular, as are tea, coffee and hot chocolate, though the tea is often made with hot rather than boiling water.

EATING OUT

A good selection of restaurants can be found in the old town area of Lourdes for those who want to try a change from the hotel food. The Tourist Office has a comprehensive list. This part of town may be reached by walking up Boulevard de la Grotte from St Michael's Gate, or by crossing the Pont Vieux and walking up Rue de la Grotte.

ESPLANADE

The Esplanade is the long stretch of path, beginning from Rosary Square, which passes the Statue of the Crowned Virgin and proceeds towards St Michael's Gate before turning back on itself towards Rosary Square. It is used for the Blessed Sacrament and Torchlight Processions.

ESPLANADE ALTAR

This is another name for the Chapel of St Bernadette, the open-air altar situated next to the ramps in the Square, on the left hand side of the Rosary Basilica.

EXHIBITIONS

A number of temporary exhibitions may be seen in the Pastoral Affairs Centre (Centre d'Animation Pastorale) on the ground floor. This Centre is close to the Permanences building and the Bookshop, on the right of the path leading into the Domaine from St Joseph's Gate. Look for signs to C.A.P.

FAMILY HOME

Eventually, after many years of misfortune, the Soubirous family made their home in the Moulin Lacade, although Bernadette herself never lived there since after the apparitions she was with the Sisters of Nevers.

GATES

There are several gates which lead into the Domaine. The two principal gates which lead from and to the hotel areas are the St Joseph's Gate, which leads from Rosary Square onto the cafes and hotels on Place Mgr Laurence, and the St Michael's Gate which is found at the east end of the Esplanade, leading over the Pont St Michel onto the Boulevard de la Grotte. At midnight all the gates are locked except the Lacets Gate which is approached up the Avenue Mgr Théas and to the right beyond the Upper Basilica.

GROTTO

This is the spot where Bernadette saw the Blessed Virgin Mary, in an alcove of the cave known as the rock of Massabielle. It is approached from the right hand side of Rosary Square and is found in between the taps and the baths. For fuller details see p.41.

GUARDS

Outside the Domaine on the streets of Lourdes, law and order is kept by the French police. Inside the Domaine there are additional officers, employed by the Oeuvre de la Grotte (the Grotto Administrative Department), who help to keep order and surveillance in the Domaine area. At all times in Lourdes, and especially when there are large crowds, beware of pickpockets.

GUIDED TOURS

Guided Tours are available from the beginning of July until the end of September each day, leaving from the statue of the Crowned Virgin. Check notices for times

HANDMAIDS

Handmaids is the word used to describe the many women who care for the sick on diocesan or national pilgrimages in Lourdes and whose male counterparts are the brancardiers. The name comes from the title given to Mary in the Angelus, the "handmaid of the Lord."

HEALTH PROVISIONS

Tourists from the European Union are only required to pay a part of any treatment or prescription costs, provided that they have an authorized E111 form from their own country of residence. Others must pay all expenses and seek any reimbursements on their return home. EU residents should follow the instructions given in the E111 leaflet.

HEMICYCLE

To the right of St Bernadette's Church, and physically part of the same building, is the Hemicycle. It is an upstairs semi-circular room which holds 500 people and can be used both for worship and for conferences.

HOSPICE OF ST BERNADETTE

The hospice is where Bernadette studied for her First Communion and where she later lived with the Sisters of Nevers after the apparitions. It is located next to the present Municipal Hospital. For more details see p.49.

HOSPITAL

Visitors to Lourdes who fall ill while on pilgrimage are usually referred to the Municipal Hospital which is situated not far from the railway station in the old town.

HOSPITALITY

The Hospitality of Our Lady of Lourdes (Hospitalité) is an association of people who serve the sick and other pilgrims in Lourdes. In addition they act as marshals at public events. Their office is under the right hand ramp of Rosary Square, Tel.05.62.94.00.27. Working in liaison with them are the various diocesan Hospitalities who also have the task of supervising the safe arrival of sick pilgrims to and from the diocese and Lourdes.

HOTELS

Lourdes comes second only to Nice in the number of hotels that it boasts. Independent travellers who wish to stay in Lourdes will find details of vacancies in the Tourist Office. Full board is almost always more economical than room only. The hotels all serve meals at the same time in order to facilitate attendance at pilgrimage events. Lunch is at 12 noon and dinner at 7pm.

INFORMATION

Besides specific offices which give information about their own particular interests, there is an general information centre just on the right after entering St Joseph's Gate. It is a rotunda-shaped building marked "Forum Information". Details of daily events in and around the Sanctuary area are posted on noticeboards close to this building. The following day's events are posted around 6pm each day.

LETTER BOXES

Most hotels are happy to look after outgoing mail and to sell you postage stamps. Around the Domaine itself there are letter boxes near the Information Points at St Joseph's Gate and St Michael's Gate, at the Acceuil Jean-Paul II and on the road level with the Upper Basilica.

LOST AND FOUND

During the pilgrimage season (Easter to November 1st) go to the Permanances (Pilgrimage Offices) near St Joseph's Gate. At other times enquire at the Forum Information.

LOURDES MAGAZINE

A monthly publication is available which gives up-to-date details of happenings in Lourdes plus articles of spiritual interest. It is available in English and may be bought from various outlets including a stall just inside the gate to the Upper Basilica opposite the Reconciliation Chapel, the entrance to St Joseph's Gate and St Michael's Gate, outside St Bernadette's Church, and from the Bookshop in the Pastoral Affairs Centre. To take out a subscription: Tel 05.62.42.79.40. The official Lourdes website is www.lourdes-france.com

MASSES

Masses are celebrated daily in most of the major languages and the times and places are posted outside the churches themselves, and on a master-timetable close to the Forum Information building. If you would like to arrange for a Mass to be celebrated for a particular intention, there is a small office behind the right hand ramps of Rosary Square which will see to this, although the waiting list is such that the Mass will almost certainly be celebrated after your departure. An International Mass, in Latin but with readings, songs and prayers in several modern languages, is held in the Underground Basilica at 9.30am every Wednesday and Sunday.

MEADOW

On the opposite side of the river to the Grotto, at the side of St Bernadette's Church, there stretches away a vast meadow (Prairie) which affords places of quiet reflection and prayer. There are a number of services found there, particularly for young people.

MEDICAL BUREAU

Situated in the Acceuil Jean-Paul II complex, the Medical Bureau deals with all the documentation relating to cures, and is the headquarters of the Lourdes International Medical Association.

MEETING ROOMS

For conferences and gatherings there are a number of halls and rooms which may be booked:

- Several rooms are available in the Forum Information building
- Salle Mgr Laurence: Avenue Mgr Théas
- Salle Notre Dame: behind the Musée Ste Bernadette
- Salle Mgr Théas: next to the Salle Notre Dame
- Conference rooms at St Bernadette's Church

MUSEUMS

There are a number of museums and exhibitions in Lourdes. Of particular note are:

Musée Ste Bernadette:

Situated close to the Missionary Pavilions on Avenue Remi-Sempé, this museum contains a presentation of the Lourdes message, various articles connected with Bernadette and a model of the place where Mary appeared in 1858.

Musée du Gemmail:

Situated at 72, Rue de la Grotte, this free museum shows sacred art in the Gemmail style of stained glass. Tel 05.62.94.13.15 for a guided tour.

Musée Grevin:

This is the waxworks museum of Lourdes containing scenes both from the life of Christ and from the story of Lourdes. It is on 87, Rue de la Grotte. Tel. 05.62.94.33.74.

Musée de Petit-Trésor:

This museum displays a 1:20 scale model of Lourdes as it was in 1858. It is to be found at the end of Avenue Peyramale by the banks of the river.

Musée du Petit-Lourdes:

On the site of the old Reconciliation Chapel and next to Salle Mgr Laurence, this Treasury Museum contains an exhibition of precious objects connected with Lourdes and the pilgrimages that have visited the shrine.

OEUVRE DE LA GROTTE

This is the administrative structure which oversees all of the services and events undertaken by the Sanctuaries. It takes its authority from the Bishop of Tarbes and Lourdes and has its office on Avenue Mgr Théas.

OFFERINGS

Anyone wishing to leave an offering for the work of the Sanctuaries, or for any other cause, may do so at the Grotto Administration building (Oeuvre de la Grotte) or in the numerous collection boxes marked "Offrandes".

PARKING

On-street parking is available at meters in designated places, and a number of parking lots are situated around Lourdes, the closest to the Domaine being the multi-storey car park on Rue Mgr Schoepfer, close to the St Joseph's Gate.

PASTORAL AFFAIRS CENTRE

The Pastoral Affairs Centre (Centre d'Animation Pastoral or C.A.P.) is the building next door to the Permanences (Pilgrimages Office) near St Joseph's Gate. It houses the Bookshop on the ground floor; on the first floor are the Language Co-ordinators; and on the top floor are the General Secretariat and the Press Office.

PAVILIONS

There is a series of pavilions at the St Michael's Gate end of Boulevard Remi Sempé and a further two under the arcades of the Esplanade. They house representatives from a wide selection of Christian Movements (including Catechumenate, Catholic Action, Missions, Vocations, Family Apostolates, Eucharistic Movement for Youth, Handicapped Fellowship, Pax Christi, Retired and Elderly, Legion of Mary, YCW, FSA and others) and provide a gathering place where people from all over the world can talk to each other, share their faith and pass on information about their particular organization.

PERMANENCES

This is the name given to the Pilgrimages Office which is found in the complex of buildings to the right after entering St Joseph's Gate. It co-ordinates the scheduling of all the various groups of pilgrims in Lourdes, and a list of daily events is posted each day and updated about 6pm.

PHOTOGRAPHY

Flash photography and video cameras can be intrusive to the liturgy, creating a sense of spectacle rather than participation, and so there may be times and places when pilgrims are asked to refrain from using them. If an official photographer takes a photograph of your group and you would like to see it before deciding whether or not to purchase it, then it is likely to be on view in one of the three accredited photographer's shops: Durand (Rue Mgr Schoepfer), Lacaze (Avenue Bernadette Soubirous) and Viron (Avenue Bernadette Soubirous).

PILGRIM'S HELP

The Entraide St Martin exists to assist pilgrims who find themselves in distress or with problems whilst in Lourdes. It is able in some circumstances to provide financial relief to those who have been robbed etc. It is this body which is able to discern whether those who beg on the streets are in genuine need or not. Those requiring further details should go to the Secours Catholique building.

PILGRIM'S SHELTER

There are facilities in the pilgrim's shelter (Abri) for leaving luggage and for picnicking. It is located at St Michael's Gate, with views of the River Gave and the St Michael's Bridge.

POLICE STATION

This is on Rue Baron-Duprat, not far from the Cachot. During the pilgrimage season there is also an office open at the Permanences building.

PRESS OFFICE

The Press Office (Bureau de Presse) provides information relevant to Lourdes, press conferences and journalist facilities. Tel. 05.62.42.78.00. It is on the top floor of the Centre d'Animation Pastorale.

PUBLIC SERVICES

- Tarbes-Ossun-Lourdes Airport: 6 miles away. Tel. 05.62.96.27.44.
- Pau Airport: 25 miles away. Tel. 05.59.33.14.03.
- Bus Station: Tel. 05.62.94.31.15.
- Railway Station: Information   Tel. 05.62.37.50.50.
                     Bookings   Tel. 05.62.94.10.47.
- Police Station: Tel.05.62.94.66.66.
- Taxi rank (at Railway Station): Tel. 05.62.94.31.30.
- Tourist Office: Tel. 05.62.42.77.40.

RAILWAY STATION

The railway station (signposted either Gare or SNCF) is on the edge of the town along the Avenue de la Gare. Regular train services connect with the wider national French rail network, and Lourdes is also convenient for Spain and Portugal via the Hendaye/Irun line. For telephone details see Public Services.

RENDEZVOUS

Although there is no official meeting point for pilgrims, many people tend to rendezvous at the statue of the Crowned Virgin in Rosary Square, since everyone who enters the Domaine from either of the two principal gates eventually has to pass this statue.

ROUTE DE BARTRÈS

On certain days the Youth Service organizes a walking trip to Bartrès for young people, a round trip of about five or six miles. For details apply to the Forum Information building or telephone the Youth Service Office on 05.62.42.79.95.

SEASON

Lourdes has two pilgrimage seasons, one active and the other less busy. The full season's timetable runs from April until October, and the winter season runs from November until March. Many of the hotels close for refurbishment during the winter season. For details of the timetables which operate in both seasons, see p.52.

SICKNESS

Anyone who falls ill during a visit to Lourdes should first consult a doctor accredited to the pilgrimage, who may decide to refer the patient. Anyone not part of a pilgrimage should consult one of the local GPs, a list of whom is available from Forum Information. People needing hospital treatment will usually be treated in the Municipal Hospital.

SPRING

The source from which Lourdes water comes is to be found behind the Grotto in the rock of Massabielle, but the water may be collected at taps which are in the wall just past the right hand ramp of the Basilica, opposite the river and before the Grotto.

STAGIAIRE

A Stagiaire is a person who has agreed to give up at least six days of their life each year (a Stage) to work under the supervision of the Lourdes Hospitality in the care of sick and disabled pilgrims.

STATIONS OF THE CROSS

There are three principal sets of Stations of the Cross in Lourdes. The main one, about 1,500 metres long with a steady climb, is to be found on Avenue Mgr Théas opposite the Crypt of the Upper Basilica, next to the Musée Trésor. A second set, which is unusual in that it has sixteen stations, is more accessible to the sick and on ground level, and is situated on the bank of the river, beyond the Grotto and the Baths. In the Underground Basilica of St Pius X there are also Stations of the Cross on the walls of the inside ramps which are accessible to the sick.

TAXIS

Taxis may be hailed on the street, or hired from the rank at the Station (SNCF) or the one at St Joseph's Gate. Alternatively you may telephone 05.62.94.31.30. You will be charged for the journey to pick you up as well as for the distance you travel to your destination. There are supplementary charges for heavy and bulky luggage (over 5kgs), and for trips to and from the station and airport.

TELEPHONES

The closest public telephones to the Domaine are:

- Outside the entrance to St Michael's Gate
- Near the old Acceuil Notre Dame
- Outside the entrance to St Joseph's Gate
- Near the Forum Information
- Close to the road entrance to the Meadow (Route de Pau)

Most French public call boxes take both coins and phone cards. The latter, useful if you are intending to make several calls, may be purchased in various denominations from the Post Office, the railway station, tobacconists (look for the diagonal-shape red cigar sign outside some shops), and from the Domaine Bookshop. Before using your hotel-room telephone it is worth checking if there is a surcharge. The public kiosks give clear directions in English on how to make international calls. For example, to phone London on 0207 123 4567, you have to dial 00 to get an international line, then 44 for England, then the London number MINUS the first "0". So the number becomes 00 44 207 123 4567.

The regional code for Lourdes is 05 but when calling from another country dial the code for France followed by 5 (omitting the 0) and then the rest of the Lourdes number.

Despite the hilly surroundings, reception for mobile digital phones is particularly good in Lourdes.

TIPPING

In most restaurants and bars you will see "Service compris" which means that the tip has already been included in the cost of the meal. On other occasions, when you think it appropriate, it is reasonable to leave a tip of 10%. If you see "T.V.A." on your bill, then this refers to Value Added Tax (VAT).

TOILETS

Public toilets are to be found in the following places:

- At the Pilgrim's Shelter near St Michael's Gate
- Under the left ramp of Rosary Square
- At St Bernadette's Church
- Near the Sanctuary Museum close to the Pavilions
- At the entrance and exit to the Stations of the Cross
- Near the Rotondes in the Meadow
- Just past the Baths going away from the Grotto

All the above, except those at the Stations of the Cross, afford access to disabled people.

TORCHLIGHT PROCESSION

This takes place each day at 8.45pm. Candles and holders may be purchased in the shops. For more details and an outline of the Service see p.154.

TOURIST OFFICE

Information on all aspects of visiting Lourdes and the surrounding area (including a useful street map of Lourdes) is available from the Office Municipale de Tourisme, Place Peyramale, in the old town centre. Tel. 05.62.42.77.40. English is spoken.

TRAFFIC DIRECTIONS

In order to encourage fairness for the traders of Lourdes, the flow of traffic is redirected every two weeks. This means that the one-way system which operates in Lourdes is reversed on the 1st and the 16th of every month, and traffic begins to drive in the opposite direction.

VOITURES

A Voiture (or Voiturette) is the bath-chair type of carriage used to transport sick pilgrims around the Sanctuaries. They are more comfortable than wheelchairs on the road surface and have the advantage of being able to form a faster and safer "snake" when several pilgrims are linked together. They may be hired at the Acceuil Marie Saint Frai, tel. 05.62.94.75.15.

WATER

The Lourdes water, coming from the Massabielle spring, may be collected at the taps which are situated behind the right hand ramp of Rosary Square, just before reaching the Grotto. Plastic bottles of varying sizes are available in the shops, but pilgrims are invited to be sparing with the amounts they take home with them.

YOUNG PEOPLE

Independent young pilgrims can use the Youth Welcome Service from July to September by going to the Forum Information building. The Rotondes (Rotundas), on the Meadow, offer the chance for quiet reflection and reading, spiritual direction and liturgical celebration each day. There is also a Youth Camp on Rue Mgr Rodhain, close to the Cité Secours St Pierre, Tel. 05.62.42.79.95. During the summer there is a popular International Mass for Young People at 8.30pm each Saturday in St Bernadette's Church. In July this is on Thursdays and in August on Saturdays.

PART THREE

"GO AND DRINK AT THE SPRING"

The Order of Mass

Mass of Our Lady of Lourdes

Mass of Mary Mother of the Church

Mass of Saint Bernadette

The Sacrament of Reconciliation

The Sacrament of Anointing of the Sick

THE ORDER OF MASS

INTRODUCTORY RITES

Greeting

When the assembly has gathered, an opening song may be sung. The ministers take their places.

All make the sign of the cross as the priest (or bishop) says:

In the name of the Father, and of the Son,
and of the Holy Spirit.
Amen.

The priest greets the people in one of the following ways:

1   The grace of our Lord Jesus Christ and the love of God
    and the fellowship of the Holy Spirit be with you all.
    And also with you.

2   The grace and peace of God our Father and the Lord
    Jesus Christ be with you.
    Blessed be God, the Father of our Lord Jesus Christ. *or*
    And also with you.

3   The Lord be with you.
    And also with you.

The priest introduces the Mass of the Day. The prayers and readings for the Mass of Our Lady of Lourdes, Mary Mother of the Church, and Saint Bernadette may be found on pp.109-120.

Penitential Rite

The priest invites the people to call on God's mercy in these or similar words:

My brothers and sisters, to prepare ourselves to celebrate the sacred mysteries, let us call to mind our sins.

After a brief silence one of the following forms is used:.

1   I confess to almighty God,
    and to you, my brothers and sisters,
    that I have sinned through my own fault
    (*all strike their breast*)
    in my thoughts and in my words,
    in what I have done,
    and in what I have failed to do;
    and I ask blessed Mary, ever virgin,
    all the angels and saints,
    and you, my brothers and sisters,
    to pray for me to the Lord our God.

    May Almighty God have mercy on us,
    forgive us our sins,
    and bring us to everlasting life.
    Amen

    Lord, have mercy.
    Lord, have mercy.

    Christ, have mercy.
    Christ, have mercy.

    Lord, have mercy.
    Lord, have mercy.

2   Lord we have sinned against you:
    Lord, have mercy.
    Lord, have mercy,

    Lord, show us your mercy and love.
    And grant us your salvation.

    May almighty God have mercy on us
    forgive us our sins,
    and bring us to everlasting life.
    Amen.

3* You were sent to heal the contrite:
    Lord, have mercy.
    Lord have mercy

You came to call sinners:
Christ, have mercy.
Christ, have mercy

You plead for us at the right hand of the Father:
Lord, have mercy.
Lord, have mercy.

May almighty God have mercy on us,
forgive us our sins,
and bring us to everlasting life.
Amen.

* Other invocations may be used.

The Gloria

At some Masses the following is sung (or said):

Glory to God in the highest,
and peace to his people on earth.
Lord God, heavenly King,
almighty God and Father,
we worship you, we give you thanks,
we praise you for your glory.
Lord Jesus Christ, only Son of the Father,
Lord God, Lamb of God,
you take away the sin of the word:
have mercy on us;
you are seated at the right hand of the Father:
receive our prayer.
For you alone are the Holy One,
you alone are the Lord,
you alone are the Most High,
Jesus Christ,
with the Holy Spirit,
in the glory of God the Father. Amen.

Opening Prayer

The priest proclaims the Opening Prayer from the Mass of the Day, at the end of which all answer: **Amen**

LITURGY OF THE WORD

The word of God is announced in a number of passages from scripture.

First Reading

This is usually taken from the Old Testament or from the Acts of the Apostles. At the end of this reading:

This is the word of the Lord

Thanks be to God

Responsorial Psalm

A psalm or canticle is sung as a reflection upon the first reading. Usually the cantor sings the verses and all join in with the refrain.

Second Reading

Taken from the New Testament, this reading is from one of the letters, from the Acts of the Apostles, or from the Book of Revelation (Apocalypse). At the end of this reading:

This is the Word of the Lord

Thanks be to God

Gospel

The Book of the Gospels may be caried in procession to the lectern, during which the Gospel Acclamation is sung.

Before the gospel:

The Lord be with you

And also with you

A reading from the Holy Gospel according to N.

Glory to you, Lord

. At the end of the gospel:

This is the gospel of the Lord

Praise to you, Lord Jesus Christ

Homily

The priest (bishop or deacon) preaches a homily which reflects upon the meaning today of the scriptures which have just been proclaimed.

Creed

We believe in one God,
    the Father, the Almighty,
    maker of heaven and earth,
    of all that is, seen and unseen.

We believe in one Lord, Jesus Christ,
    the only Son of God,
    eternally begotten of the Father,
    God from God, Light from Light,
    true God from true God,
    begotten, not made,
    of one Being with Father.
    Through him all things were made.
    For us men and for our salvation
    he came down from heaven: *(all bow)*
    by the power of the Holy Spirit
    he became Incarnate from the Virgin Mary,
    and was made man.
    For our sake he was crucified under Pontius Pilate;
    he suffered death and was buried.
    On the third day he rose again
    in accordance with the Scriptures;
    he ascended into heaven
    and seated at the right of the Father.
    He will come again in glory
    to judge the living and the dead,
    and his kingdom will have no end.

We believe in the Holy Spirit, the Lord, the giver of life,
    who proceeds from the Father and the Son.
    With the Father and the Son
    he is worshipped and glorified.
    He has spoken through the Prophets.

We believe in one holy catholic and apostolic Church.
We acknowledge one baptism
for the forgiveness of sins.
We look for the resurrection of the dead.
and the life of the world to come. Amen.

Prayer of the Faithful

In this prayer the whole assembly prays for the needs of the world, the Church and the local community.

After an invitation, there follows a series of petitions. These are answered by a response which may be sung or said. A prayer by the priest concludes this and all reply:

Amen.

LITURGY OF THE EUCHARIST

Having listened to God's invitation in the scriptures, we now follow Christ's command at the Last Supper to 'take, bless, break and eat' in memory of him.

Preparation of the Gifts

A collection may be taken and brought along with the gifts of bread and wine to the altar. A hymn or song may accompany this procession and the preparation of the altar. If there is no hymn the priest may say the prayers aloud and the people make the responses given here.

Blessed are you, Lord, God of all creation.
Through your goodness we have this bread to offer,
which earth has given and human hands have made.
It will become for us the bread of life.
Blessed be God forever.

Blessed are you, Lord, God of all creation.
Through your goodness we have this wine to offer,
fruit of the vine and work of human hands.
It will become our spiritual drink.
Blessed be God forever.

Pray, brethren, that my sacrifice and yours
may be acceptable to God the almighty Father.
May the Lord accept the sacrifice at your hands,
for the praise and glory of his name,
for our good, and the good of all his Church.

Prayer over the Gifts

This prayer is taken from the Mass of the Day. At the end all answer:

Amen

The Eucharistic Prayer

In the eucharistic prayer the whole assembly unites to praise and give
thanks to God and to offer sacrifice

Eucharistic Prayer II

Preface

The Lord be with you.
And also with you.

Lift up your hearts.
We lift them up to the Lord.

Let us give thanks to the Lord our God.
It is right to give him thanks and praise.

The following preface may be used, or one taken from pp.109-120 or
elsewhere

Father, it is our duty and our salvation,
always and everywhere
to give you thanks
through your beloved Son, Jesus Christ.
He is the Word through whom you made the universe,
the Saviour you sent to redeem us.
By the power of the Holy Spirit
he took flesh and was born of the Virgin Mary,
For our sake he opened his arms on the cross;
he put an end to death

and revealed the resurrection.
In this he fulfilled your will
and won for you a holy people.
And so we join the angels and the saints
in proclaiming your glory
as we sing (say):

**Holy, holy, holy Lord, God of power and might,
heaven and earth are full of your glory.
Hosanna in the highest.**

**Blessed is he who comes in the name of the Lord.
Hosanna in the highest.**

Lord, you are holy indeed,
the fountain of all holiness.
Let your Spirit come upon these gifts to make them holy,
so that they may become for us
the body + and blood of our Lord, Jesus Christ.

Before he was given up to death,
a death he freely accepted,
he took bread and gave you thanks.
He broke the bread,
gave it to his disciples, and said:
**Take this, all of you, and eat it:
this is my body which will be given up for you.**

When supper was ended, he took the cup.
Again he gave you thanks and praise,
gave the cup to his disciples, and said:
**Take this, all of you, and drink from it:
this is the cup of my blood,
the blood of the new and everlasting covenant.
It will be shed for you and for all
so that sins may be forgiven.
Do this in memory of me.**

Memorial Acclamation

Let us proclaim the mystery of faith:

One of the following may be sung (or said):

1   Christ has died,
    Christ is risen,
    Christ will come again.

2   Dying you destroyed our death,
    rising you restored our life.
    Lord Jesus, come in glory.

3   When we eat this bread and drink this cup,
    we proclaim your death, Lord Jesus,
    until you come in glory.

4   Lord, by your cross and resurrection
    you have set us free.
    You are the Saviour of the world.

In memory of his death and resurrection,
we offer you, Father, this life-giving bread,
this saving cup.
We thank you for counting us worthy
to stand in your presence and serve you.
May all of us who share in the body and blood of Christ
be brought together in unity by the Holy Spirit.

Lord, remember your Church throughout the world;
make us grow in love,
together with N. our Pope,
N. our bishop, and all the clergy.
In Masses for the Dead, the following may be added:

(Remember N., whom you have called from this life.
In baptism he (she) died with Christ:
may he (she) also share his resurrection.)

Remember our brothers and sisters
who have gone to their rest
in the hope of rising again;
bring them and all the departed
into the light of your presence.

Have mercy on us all;
make us worthy to share eternal life

with Mary, the virgin Mother of God,
with the apostles, and with all the saints
who have done your will throughout the ages.
May we praise you in union with them,
and give you glory
through your Son, Jesus Christ.

Through him,
with him,
in him.
in the unity of the Holy Spirit,
all glory and honour is yours,
almighty Father,
for ever and ever.
Amen.

Eucharistic Prayer III

Father, you are holy indeed,
and all creation rightly gives you praise.
All life, all holiness comes from you
through your Son, Jesus Christ our Lord,
by the working of the Holy Spirit.
From age to age you gather a people to yourself,
so that from east to west
a perfect offering may be made
to the glory of your name.

And so, Father, we bring you these gifts.
We ask you to make them holy by the power of your Spirit.
that they may become the body + and blood
of your Son, our Lord Jesus Christ,
at whose command we celebrate this eucharist.

On the night he was betrayed,
he took bread and gave you thanks and praise.
He broke the bread, gave it to his disciples, and said:
Take this, all of you, and eat it:
this is my body which will be given up for you.

When supper was ended, he took the cup.
Again he gave you thanks and praise,
gave the cup to his disciples, and said:
Take this, all of you, and drink from it:
this is the cup of my blood,
the blood of the new and everlasting covenant.
It will be shed for you and for all
so that sins may be forgiven.
Do this in memory of me.

Memorial Acclamation

Let us proclaim the mystery of faith:

One of the following may be sung (or said):

1   Christ has died,
    Christ is risen,
    Christ will come again.

2   Dying you destroyed our death,
    rising you restored our life.
    Lord Jesus, come in glory.

3   When we eat this bread and drink this cup,
    we proclaim your death, Lord Jesus,
    until you come in glory.

4   Lord, by your cross and resurrection
    you have set us free.
    You are the Saviour of the world.

Father, calling to mind the death your Son endured
   for our salvation,
his glorious resurrection and ascension into heaven,
and ready to greet him when he comes again,
we offer you in thanksgiving this holy and living sacrifice.

Look with favour on your Church's offering,
and see the Victim whose death has reconciled
   us to yourself.
Grant that we, who are nourished by his body and blood,
may be filled with his Holy Spirit,
and become one body, one spirit in Christ.

May he make us an everlasting gift to you
and enable us to share in the inheritance of your saints,
with Mary, the virgin Mother of God;
with the apostles, the martyrs,
Saint N. *(the saint of the day)* and all your saints,
on whose constant intercession we rely for help.

Lord, may this sacrifice,
which has made our peace with you,
advance the peace and salvation of all the world.
Strengthen in faith and love your pilgrim Church on earth;
your servant, Pope N., our bishop N., and all the bishops,
with the clergy and the entire people your Son
    has gained for you.
Father, hear the prayers of the family you have gathered
    here before you.
In mercy and love unite all your children
    wherever they may be.
Welcome into your kingdom
    our departed brothers and sisters,
and all who have left this world in your friendship.
We hope to enjoy for ever the vision of your glory,
through Christ our Lord, from whom all good things come.

Through him,
with him,
in him.
in the unity of the Holy Spirit,
all glory and honour is yours,
almighty Father,
for ever and ever. **Amen.**

COMMUNION RITE

The Lord's Prayer

The priest invites everyone in these or similar words to join in the Lord's Prayer:

Let us pray with confidence to the Father
in the words our Saviour gave us:

Our Father, who art in heaven…

Deliver us, Lord, from every evil,
and grant us peace in our day.
In your mercy keep us free from sin
and protect us from all anxiety
as we wait in joyful hope
for the coming of our Saviour, Jesus Christ.
For the kingdom, the power and the glory are yours, now and forever.

Rite of Peace

Lord Jesus Christ, you said to your apostles;
I leave you peace, my peace I give you.
Look not on our sins, but on the faith of your Church,
and grant us the peace and unity of your kingdom
where you live for ever and ever.
Amen.

The peace of the Lord be with you always
And also with you.

Let us offer each other the sign of peace.

All make a sign of peace, according to local custom.

The priest breaks the consecrated bread in preparation for Communion, in accordance with the action of Christ at the Last Supper.

Meanwhile the following is sung (or said):

Lamb of God, you take away the sins of the world:
    have mercy on us.
Lamb of God, you take away the sins of the world:
    have mercy on us.
Lamb of God, you take away the sins of the world:
    grant us peace.

Communion

The priest invites all to Communion with these or similar words:

This is the Lamb of God
who takes away the sins of the world.
Happy are those who are called to his supper.

Lord, I am not worthy to receive you,
but only say the word and I shall be healed.

A song or hymn may be sung as people come forward in procession for Communion.

The priest or other minister offers the host and chalice to each communicant:

The body of Christ
Amen.

The blood of Christ
Amen

After Communion ,a period of silence may be observed, or a song or hymn may be sung.

Prayer after Communion

This prayer is taken from the Mass of the Day. At the end all answer:

Amen

Concluding Rite

Blessing and Dismissal

Any brief announcements may be made. Then the priest says:

The Lord be with you.
And also with you.

May almighty God bless you,
the Father, and the Son, + and the Holy Spirit.
Amen.

The priest (or deacon) dismisses the assembly in the following or similar words:

The Mass is ended, go in peace   *or*

Go in the peace of Christ   *or*

Go in peace to love and serve the Lord.
Thanks be to God.

The celebration may conclude with a song or hymn.

MASS OF OUR LADY OF LOURDES

The following prayers, readings and chants may be used at this Mass, or others may be chosen from the Roman Missal and Lectionary.

OPENING PRAYER

O God,
by the Virgin's Immaculate Conception,
you prepared a fitting dwelling-place for your Son.
We humbly ask you that we,
who are recalling her apparition here at Lourdes,
may obtain through her prayers all that we need
for the well-being of soul and body.
We ask this through our Lord Jesus Christ, your Son,
who lives and reigns with you and the Holy Spirit,
one God for ever and ever.
Amen.

FIRST READING

A reading from the Book of the Apocalypse (21:1-7)

Then I, John, saw a new heaven and a new earth; for the first heaven and the first earth had passed away, and the sea was no more.

And I saw the holy city, the new Jerusalem, coming down out of heaven from God, prepared as a bride adorned for her husband.

And I heard a loud voice from the throne saying, "See, the home of God is among mortals. He will dwell with them as their God; they will be his peoples, and God himself will be with them; he will wipe every tear from their eyes. Death will be no more; mourning and crying and pain will be no more, for the first things have passed away."

And the One who was seated on the throne said, "See, I am making all things new." Also he said, "Write this, for these words are trustworthy and true."

The he said to me, "It is done! I am the Alpha and the

Omega, the beginning and the end. To the thirsty I will give water as a gift from the spring of the water of life. Those who conquer will inherit these things, and I will be their God and they will be my children."

RESPONSORIAL PSALM (Psalm 97:1-4)

R. **Sing a new song to the Lord**
  for he has worked wonders.

1 Sing a new song to the Lord
  for he has worked wonders.
  His right hand and his holy arm
  have brought salvation.

2 The Lord has made know his salvation;
  has shown his justice to the nations.
  He has remembered his truth and love
  for the house of Israel.

3 All the ends of the earth have seen
  the salvation of our God.
  Shout to the Lord all the earth,
  ring out your joy.

GOSPEL ACCLAMATION

Alleluia, Alleluia!
Blessed is the Virgin Mary
who treasured the word of God
and pondered it in her heart.
Alleluia!

(*During Lent*)

Glory and praise to you, O Christ!
They are happy who dwell in your house, O Lord,
for ever singing your praise.
Glory and praise to you, O Christ!

GOSPEL

A reading from the holy Gospel according to Luke (1:26-38)

In the sixth month the angel Gabriel was sent by God to a town in Galilee called Nazareth, to a virgin engaged to a man whose name was Joseph, of the house of David. The virgin's name was Mary.

And he came to her and said, "Greetings, favoured one! The Lord is with you." But she was much perplexed by his words and pondered what sort of greeting this might be.

The angel said to her, "Do not be afraid, Mary, for you have found favour with God. And now, you will conceive in your womb and bear a son, and you will name him Jesus. He will be great, and will be called the Most High, and the Lord God will give to him the throne of his ancestor David. He will reign over the house of Jacob for ever, and of his kingdom there will be no end."

Mary said to the angel, "How can this be, since I am a virgin?" The angel said to her, "The Holy Spirit will come upon you, and the power of the Most High will overshadow you; therefore the child to be born will be holy; he will be called Son of God. And now your relative Elizabeth in her old age has also conceived a son; and this is the sixth month for her who was said to be barren. For nothing will be impossible with God."

Then Mary said, "Here am I, the servant of the Lord; let it be with me according to your word." Then the angel departed from her.

PRAYER OVER THE GIFTS

By your gracious mercy, Lord,
and at the intercession of the glorious
and immaculate virgin, Mary,
let this offering bring us prosperity and peace, now and for evermore.
Amen.

PREFACE

Father, all-powerful and ever-living God,
we do well always and everywhere to give you thanks.
You allowed no stain of Adam's sin
to touch the Virgin Mary.
Full of grace, she was to be a worthy mother of your Son,
your sign of favour to the Church at its beginning,
and the promise of its perfection as the bride of Christ,
radiant in beauty.
Purest of virgins, she was to bring forth your Son,
the innocent lamb who takes away our sins.
You chose her from all women to be our advocate with you
and our pattern of holiness.
In our joy we sing to your glory
with all the choirs of angels:

PRAYER AFTER COMMUNION

We who have feasted on this heavenly banquet
humbly ask you, Lord,
that having given us an intercessor and protectress
in your Son's immaculate mother,
you will reward us pilgrims
with everlasting happiness in heaven.
We ask this through Christ our Lord.
Amen.

MASS OF MARY
MOTHER OF THE CHURCH

The following prayers, readings and chants may be used at this Mass, or others may be chosen from the Roman Missal and Lectionary.

OPENING PRAYER

Father of mercies,
your only Son, hanging on the cross,
gave us his virgin mother, Mary,
to be our mother also.
Under her loving care
may her children grow daily in holiness,
so that all mankind
may see in your Church
the mother of all nations.
We ask this through our Lord Jesus Christ, your Son,
who lives and reigns with you and the Holy Spirit,
one God, for ever and ever.
Amen.

FIRST READING

A reading from the Acts of the Apostles (1:12-14)

The Apostles returned to Jerusalem from the mount called Olivet, which is near Jerusalem, a Sabbath's day's journey away. When they had entered the city, they went to the room upstairs where they were staying, Peter and John, and James, and Andrew, Philip and Thomas, Bartholomew and Matthew, James son of Alphaeus, and Simon the Zealot, and Judas son of James. All these were constantly devoting themselves to prayer, together with certain women, including Mary the mother of Jesus, as well as their brothers.

RESPONSORIAL PSALM (Luke 1:46-55)

**R. Blessed is the Virgin Mary
who bore the son of the eternal Father.**

1 My soul glorifies the Lord,
my spirit rejoices in God, my saviour.

2 He looks on his servant in her nothingness,
henceforth all ages will call me blessed.
The almighty works marvels for me,
Holy his name!

3 His mercy is from age to age,
on those who fear him.
He puts forth his arm in strength
and scatters the proud-hearted.

4 He casts the mighty from their thrones
and raises the lowly.
He fills the starving with good things,
sends the rich away empty.

5 He protects Israel, his servant,
remembering his mercy,
the mercy promised to our fathers,
to Abraham and his sons for ever.

GOSPEL ACCLAMATION

Alleluia, Alleluia!
Happy are those who hear the word of God, and keep it.
Alleluia!

(During Lent)

Glory and praise to you, O Christ!
They are happy who dwell in your house, O Lord,
for ever singing your praise.
Glory and praise to you, O Christ!

GOSPEL

A reading from the holy Gospel according to John
(19:25-27)

Standing by the cross of Jesus were his mother, and his
mother's sister, Mary the wife of Clopas, and Mary

Magdalene. When Jesus saw his mother and the disciple whom he loved standing beside her, he said to his mother, "Woman, here is your son." Then he said to the disciple, "Here is your mother." And from that hour the disciple took her into his own home.

PRAYER OVER THE GIFTS

Lord,
accept our offerings,
and make them the sacrament of our salvation:
By its power
warm our hearts with the love
of the Virgin Mary, Mother of the Church,
and bring us closer to her
in sharing your redeeming love.
We ask this through Christ our Lord.
Amen.

PREFACE

Father, all-powerful and ever-living God,
we do well always and everywhere to give you thanks
and, as we honour the Blessed Virgin Mary,
to offer you fitting praise.
She received your Word
in the purity of her heart,
and conceived him
in her virgin's womb;
she gave birth to her Creator,
and watched over the Church
at its first beginning.
She accepted God's parting gift of love
as she stood beside the Cross,
and so became the Mother of all the living,
her children brought to new life
through the death of her Son.
One in prayer with the apostles
as they waited for the promised Gift of your Spirit,

she became the perfect pattern of the Church at prayer.
Raised to the glory of heaven,
she cares for the pilgrim Church
with a mother's love,
following its progress homewards
until the day of the Lord dawns in splendour.
Now, with all the saints and angels,
we praise you for ever:

PRAYER AFTER COMMUNION

Lord,
we have received the promise and foretaste
of the fullness of redemption:
we pray that your Church,
through the intercession of the Virgin Mother,
may proclaim the Gospel to all nations,
and fill the whole world
with the presence of your Spirit.
We ask this through Christ our Lord.
Amen.

MASS OF SAINT BERNADETTE

The following prayers, readings and chants may be used at this Mass, or others may be chosen from the Roman Missal and Lectionary.

OPENING PRAYER

Father,
rewarder of the humble,
you blessed Saint Bernadette
with charity and patience.
May her prayer help us,
and her example inspire us
to carry our cross and to love you always.
We ask this through our Lord Jesus Christ, your Son,
who lives and reigns with you and the Holy Spirit,
one God for ever and ever.
Amen.

FIRST READING

A reading from the first letter of St Paul to the Corinthians (1:26-31)

Consider your own call, brothers and sisters: not many of you were wise by human standards, not many were powerful, not many were of noble birth. But God chose what is foolish in the world to shame the wise; God chose what is weak in the world to shame the strong; God chose what is low and despised in the world, things that are not, to reduce to nothing things that are, so that no one might boast in the presence of God. He is the source of your life in Christ Jesus, who became for us wisdom from God, and righteousness and sanctification and redemption, in order that, as it is written, "Let the one who boasts, boast in the Lord."

RESPONSORIAL PSALM (Psalm 148: 1-2, 11-14)

R. Young men and maidens
     praise the name of the Lord.

1 Praise the Lord from the heavens,
  praise him in the heights.
  Praise him, all his angels,
  praise him, all his host.

2 All earth's kings and peoples,
  earth's princes and rulers;
  young men and maidens,
  old men together with children.

3 Let them praise the name of the Lord
  for he alone is exalted.
  The splendour of his name
  reaches beyond heaven and earth.

4 He exalts the strength of his people.
  He is the praise of all his saints,
  of the sons of Israel,
  of the people to whom he comes close.

GOSPEL ACCLAMATION

Alleluia, Alleluia!
Happy are the poor in spirit;
theirs is the kingdom of heaven.
Alleluia!

(*During Lent*)

Glory and praise to you, O Christ!
They are happy who dwell in your house, O Lord,
for ever singing your praise.
Glory and praise to you, O Christ!

GOSPEL

A reading from the holy Gospel according to Matthew
(11:25-30)

At that time Jesus said, "I thank you, Father, Lord of heaven and earth, because you have hidden these things from the wise and the intelligent and have revealed them to infants;

yes, Father, for such was your gracious will. All things have been handed over to me by my Father; and no one knows the Son except the Father, and no one knows the Father except the Son and anyone to whom the Son chooses to reveal him.

Come to me, all you that are weary and are carrying heavy burdens, and I will give you rest. Take my yoke upon you, and learn from me; for I am gentle and humble in heart, and you will find rest for your souls. For my yoke is easy, and my burden is light."

PRAYER OVER THE GIFTS

Lord,
receive the gifts your people bring to you
in honour of your saints.
By the eucharist we celebrate,
may we progress towards salvation.
We ask this through Christ our Lord.
Amen.

PREFACE

Father, all-powerful and ever-living God,
we do well always and everywhere to give you thanks.
You are glorified in your saints,
for their glory is the crowning of your gifts.
In their lives on earth
you give us an example.
In our communion with them
you give us their friendship.
In their prayer for the Church
you give us strength and protection.
This great company of witnesses
spurs us on to victory,
to share their prize of everlasting glory,
through Jesus Christ our Lord.
With the angels and archangels
and the whole company of saints
we sing our unending hymn of praise:

PRAYER AFTER COMMUNION

Lord, we receive your gifts
at this celebration in honour of Saint Bernadette.
May they free us from sin
and strengthen us by your grace.
We ask this through Christ our Lord.
Amen.

THE SACRAMENT OF RECONCILIATION

The sacrament of reconciliation, sometimes also called penance or confession, is a celebration of Christ's victory over sin by his death on the cross. Our creed asserts that Christians are baptized for the forgiveness of sins. In its ministry of reconciliation the Church makes present that redeeming power of Christ's love, and proclaims forgiveness for sins committed after baptism.

Sin is forgiven by God in many different ways: by prayer, by self-denial, by good works, by participating in the eucharist etc. But the sacrament of reconciliation is the privileged moment in which the Church guarantees God's pardon to the sinner who truly repents.

A pilgrimage to Lourdes is an especially good time to celebrate this sacrament. Not only does it re-echo Our Lady's revelation to Bernadette of "Penance, Penance, Penance", but it continues the long historical link between pilgrimages and conversion. A pilgrimage is a journey which takes us closer to God, and the sacrament of penance is a sign of our continual journey out of darkness and into light.

Pilgrimages are occasions for taking stock. By engaging in something out of the ordinary, by standing back from our run of the mill routine and travelling to Mary's shrine, we have the chance to look at the priorities which govern our daily existence. We have the leisure to ask whether there are areas of our life which need attention if they are to become more productive and expressive of God's will.

So pilgrimages invite us to change for the better. It would be a sad pilgrim who returned home the same person. Just as a pilgrimage is heightened by travelling with other pilgrims, so too the sacrament of penance is more fully understood when celebrated communally. The pilgrim Church gathers together to recognize that our individual sins do damage the whole Body of Christ, and that the reconciliation promised by the sacrament is with God and with each other. We confess to almighty God and to our brothers and sisters.

For this reason, most pilgrimages offer the opportunity to celebrate the sacrament of reconciliation communally. This would be the rite most favoured by the Church. In this case a complete and self-contained rite, usually including individual confession of sin, is generally prepared by those leading the pilgrimage.

When, for whatever reason, a pilgrim is celebrating this sacrament individually, perhaps at the Reconciliation Chapel, personal preparation is essential if the occasion is not to be seen as a merely casual act, but rather as a genuine encounter with the reconciling Christ.

An outline of the individual rite can be found below, but personal preparation demands first that we pause to recognize two important factors: the call to conversion and our need to prepare a way for God through an examination of conscience.

THE CALL TO CONVERSION

Confession should never frighten us. It is not so much an appearance before a judge who is about to sentence us, as a return home to a God who wants to be close to us. The best word we can use to describe our God is love. Confession is the loving encounter between us and God. It is about hope, acceptance and a fresh start. In this sacrament we allow God to love us.

God's forgiveness to the repentant sinner is unconditional. We cannot earn it; it has already been won for us by Christ's death and resurrection. The Holy Spirit is our pledge of God's serious intent in reconciling us to him and to each other.

The call to conversion is found in God's word in scripture. We are called to change our minds, to change our hearts, and to open ourselves to the living challenge which God lays down before us:

I am the Lord your God,
who brought you out of the land of Egypt,

out of the house of slavery.
Do not have other gods besides me.   (Ex 20:1-3)

Listen, Israel: Yahweh, our God, is the one Lord.
You shall love him with all your heart,
with your full soul,
and with your whole strength.
Engrave on your hearts
the commandments I urge on you today.
Repeat them again and again to your children;
speak of them when you are at home and when you travel,
when you go to bed and when you get up.
Fasten them on your hand as a sign
and on your forehead as a circlet.
Carve them on your doorposts at home
and on your city gates.   (Deut 20:4-9)

Take your wrong-doing out of my sight.
Put an end to evil and learn to do good.
Search for justice,
give hope to the oppressed;
be just towards the orphans
and defend the widows.
Come now, let us talk this over:
Although your sins are like scarlet,
they shall become as white as snow;
although they are crimson red,
they shall become as white as wool.   (Is 1:16-18)

The Lord says:
Come back to me now with all your heart,
with fasting, weeping, mourning.
Tear your heart, not your clothes;
turn to the Lord your God again,
for he is rich in tenderness and compassion,
slow to anger and full of kindness,
ready to relent.
Who knows? Probably he will turn again and relent.
Maybe he will leave a blessing as he passes. (Joel 2:12-14)

You have been told what is good
and what the Lord asks of you.
Only this:
that you act justly,
that you love tenderly,
that you walk humbly with your God.   (Micah 6:8)

At the time Christ died for us we were still sinners.
It is not easy to die for someone, even for a good person.
Although for a very worthy person
perhaps people would give their life.
But what proves that God loves us
is that Christ died for us while we were still sinners.
And having died to make us just and holy,
is it likely that he would now fail
to save us from God's anger?
From being enemies, we have become at peace with God,
through the death of his Son.
Surely now, with much more reason,
we may count on being saved by the life of his Son?
Not only that;
we feel secure in God because of Christ Jesus,
through whom we have already been reconciled. (Rom 5:6-11)

Be doers of (God's) word and not just hearers.
To hear the word and not obey it
is like looking at your face in the mirror
and then, after a brief glance,
going off and forgetting what you looked like.
But those who fix their gaze on the perfect law of freedom
and hold onto it, not listening and then forgetting,
but putting it into practice,
will be happy in all that they do. (James 1:22-25)

If we claim that we have no sin in us,
we are deceiving ourselves and the truth is not in us.
But if we confess our sins,
God who is faithful and just
will forgive us our sins and cleanse us from our wrong-doings.

To say we have never sinned is to make God a liar,
and it shows that his word is not in us.   (1 Jn 1:8-10)

Jesus taught them:
Blessed are those who have the spirit of the poor:
for theirs is the kingdom of heaven.
Blessed are the gentle:
for they shall inherit the earth.
Blessed are those who mourn:
for they shall be comforted.
Blessed are those who hunger and thirst for justice:
for they shall be satisfied.
Blessed are the merciful:
for they shall find mercy.
Blessed are those with a pure heart:
for they shall see God.
Blessed are those who work for peace,
for they shall be called children of God.
Blessed are those who suffer persecution
for justice's sake:
for theirs is the kingdom of heaven.
Blessed are you when people insult you
and persecute you
and speak all kinds of calumny against you
because you are my followers.
Rejoice and be glad,
because your reward will be great in heaven.
This is just how they persecuted the prophets
before you.   (Mt 5:2-12)

Jesus said to them:
Pay attention to what you hear.
Whatever amount you give,
that will you receive, and still more.
For to those who produce something
more will be given.
But, from those who do not produce anything,
even what they have will be taken away.   (Mk 4:24-25)

Jesus said:
Who among you, if he has a hundred sheep and loses one,
will not leave the ninety-nine in the wilderness
and go after the missing one until he finds it?
And finding it,
will he not take it joyfully home on his shoulders
and call his friends and neighbours together saying,
"Celebrate with me,
for I have found my sheep that was lost"?
In the same way, I tell you,
there will be more rejoicing in heaven
over one repentant sinner
than over ninety-nine upright people
who have no need to repent.   (L*k* 15:4-7)

Jesus said to them:
Peace be with you.
Just as the Father sent me,
so I am sending you.
When he had said this he breathed on them, saying:
If you forgive anyone's sins they are forgiven;
if you retain anyone's sins they are retained. (J*n* 20:21-23)

EXAMINATION OF CONSCIENCE

When we examine our conscience we are looking for more than a list of rules that we have broken. We are seeking to look deeper into ourselves, into our very being, and to ask, in the light of God's word, how we can change and become more receptive to the life of grace working within us.

So we ask three questions:

✠   WHAT have I done or not done?

✠   WHY have I acted in that way?

✠   HOW can I begin to cooperate with God's grace?

It is so easy to get stuck with the first question, and simply make a list of wrong-doings which we recount every time we go to confession. It is important that we know WHAT we have done or not done, but a truly fruitful celebration of the sacrament demands that we go deeper.

Why do I act as I do? Are there habits that I have got into, or out of, which cause me to behave this way? Are there situations that I should really distance myself from, or people who easily lead me astray? Are there aspects of my lifestyle which invite trouble? It is the question WHY which can set us on the way to avoiding our most sinful actions.

When we have honestly tried to see why we behave as we do, we can start to find out HOW to avoid falling back again into our old ways. The new sense of purpose that this gives us is part of the hope that we can really amend our lives and let Christ be at the centre of our decisions. It offers us an alternative way of living.

The following simple examination of conscience is designed to help us go beyond the surface, beyond a mere list of sins, to ask the deeper question, What sort of person am I becoming and how can I nurture God's life within me?

No examination of conscience can be rushed. Take your time; ask for God's help, and accept it as a time of prayer.

(*Other similar examinations of conscience are available on leaflets in the Reconciliation Chapel.*)

SIMPLE EXAMINATION OF CONSCIENCE

Jesus said,

> "*The first commandment is `Hear, O Israel, the Lord our God is the one Lord, and you must love the Lord your God with all your heart, with your full soul, with all your mind and your whole strength.' The second is this: `You must love your neighbour as yourself.'*" (Mk 12:29-31)

All the commandments, then, are summed up in:

☩ Love of God

☩ Love of neighbour

☩ Love of self

☩ Love of God

Is God someone distant or a real part of my life?

Do I pray regularly and join the community in its Sunday worship?

Do I read God's word and try to understand what it demands of me?

Is Christ central to my decisions?

Am I conscious of the promptings of the Holy Spirit?

Have I used the name of God or Christ as a swear-word?

Are there any false gods in my life: sex, money, ambition?

☩ Love of Neighbour

Do I care about other people, or do I just stick to my friends?

Do I contribute to the happiness of my family or detract from it?

Am I a good parent?

Have I faithfully kept my marriage vows to my husband or wife?

What kind of Christian example do I give to others at work?

Do I put in a fair day's work or pay a fair wage?

Do I take a public stand on moral and social issues?

Am I concerned for the sick, the poor, those in prison?

Do I gossip or spread rumours about people?

Have I stolen money or goods?

Do I encourage people or do I use them for my own purposes?

Have I been verbally or physically violent towards people?

Are there people whom I refuse to forgive?

✠ **Love of Self**

Do I thank God for the wonder of my being?

Do I always follow my own conscience?

Have I tried to grow in my understanding of faith?

Have I abused my body by eating or drinking too much?

Do I use my body impurely as an object of sexual gratification?

Have I read or watched material which offends human decency?

Do I indulge in pride and boastfulness?

Have I borne sickness and trials with patience?

Am I lazy, closed-minded or slothful?

Do I give in to disappointment and self-pity?

Am I a truthful person in my words and in my dealings?

INDIVIDUAL CELEBRATION OF THE SACRAMENT

1 Personal Preparation

It is useful to spend some time in quiet prayer before confessing one's sins. Ideally it is the word of God in scripture which should be the spring board for our examination of conscience. God's word convicts us, yet at the same time it gives us hope in the divine mercy promised us. Reading quietly a suitable passage from scripture sets the tone for what is to follow.

Some brief scripture passages and an examination of conscience can be found on pp.122-129. At the Reconciliation Chapel in Lourdes there are leaflets in different languages which will also help with this personal preparation.

2 Greeting and Welcome

The penitent and the priest make the sign of the cross together:

In the name of the Father.
and of the Son,
and of the Holy Spirit. Amen.

May the Lord Jesus welcome you.
He came to call sinners, not the just.
Have confidence in him. (Luke 5:32)

The penitent can begin by saying something like "**Bless me, Father, for I have sinned…**" or any other phrase which seems appropriate. It can be helpful for the priest to know something about the penitent's state of life, marital status, profession, age, frequency of going to confession etc. It gives him a better opportunity to offer practical advice and spiritual counsel.

3 The Word of God

The penitent should tell the priest about the scripture passage he or she has read before coming to confess. If time permits, the passage can be read by priest or penitent. Alternatively the priest may read or quote from memory a suitable passage.

4 Confession of Sins

In the light of God's word, the penitent confesses those sins which have been committed. An integral confession includes not only things we have done, and things we have neglected to do, but also those underlying trends in our life which bring us closer to God or make us weaker in our faith. We are asked to uncover not just what we have done but what sort of people we are. Sin is more than breaking a law; it is the slackness which can lead to the eventual breakdown of our relationship with God.

When the penitent has finished confessing, the priest responds to what has been said and tries to offer suitable advice and encouragement. He proposes a penance or satisfaction which should correspond with what the penitent has confessed. The purpose of this penance or satisfaction is not only to make up for the past, but to help the penitent amend his or her future life. So it may be a prayer, an act of mercy, self-denial, service of one's neighbour etc.

5 Prayer of Sorrow

The priest invites the penitent to express sorrow for sins committed. This could be a familiar Act of Contrition, the penitent's own words, or the following or similar prayer:

Father, I am not worthy
to be called your child.
By my sins
I have wandered from your love
and have chosen ways
which do not bring me life.
Lord, I acknowledge my guilt
and my sin is always before me.
By your Son's dying and rising
blot out my offence,
and bring me to the joy
of serving you once more,
in the family of your Church,
for the glory of your name.

6. Sacramental Absolution

The priest extends his hands over the penitent's head saying:

God, the Father of mercies,
through the death and resurrection of his Son
has reconciled the world to himself
and sent the Holy Spirit among us
for the forgiveness of sins;
through the ministry of the Church
may God give you pardon and peace,
and I absolve you from your sins
in the name of the Father, and of the Son ✛,
and of the Holy Spirit.

The penitent responds. **Amen.**

7 Praise of God and Dismissal

The priest uses a simple phrase or acclamation of praise and dismisses the penitent, who replies with "Amen" or "Thanks be to God", before leaving the place where the sacrament has been celebrated. For example:

> Your sins are forgiven; go in peace.
> **Thanks be to God.**

8. Thanksgiving for the Sacrament

It is always recommended that upon returning to the church or chapel, the penitent should take a few moments to reflect on what has taken place during the sacrament, and should make a brief act of thanksgiving before leaving. The following prayer may be found suitable for this purpose:

> Happy are those whose offence is forgiven
> whose sin is wiped away.
> Blessed are those to whom the Lord imputes no guilt,
> in whose spirit is found no deceit.
> When I kept my sin secret, my body wasted away.
> I groaned all day long;
> your hand lay heavy upon me
> by night and by day.
> But now I have acknowledged my sins,
> and uncovered my guilt before you.
> I said to myself:
> "I will confess my wrong to the Lord."
> And now, Lord, you have forgiven my sin
> and removed all my guilt.
> I give you thanks, my God, with all my heart,
> and glorify your name, O Lord, for ever;
> for your great love to me has been constant,
> and you have saved me from the depths.
> Blessed be God who did not reject my prayer,
> nor withold his love from me.

(*Based on Pss.31, 65 and 85*)

THE SACRAMENT OF
ANOINTING OF THE SICK

It is clear from reading the gospels that much of Jesus's ministry was taken up with those who suffered sickness or disease. Time after time the evangelists recount stories of how people were brought to him so that he could cure them. These included disabilities which would normally be lifelong, like blindness or leprosy, as well as those ailments which afflict us temporarily but leave us debilitated and sometimes downhearted.

> *That evening they brought him many who were possessed by devils. He cast out the spirits with a word and cured all who were sick. This was to fulfil the prophecy of Isaiah: He took our sicknesses away and carried our diseases for us.* (Mt 8.16-17)

Whenever Jesus cured a person, it was always as a sign of something else. The visible cure was a testimony that he had restored the person to a wholeness which often could not be seen. He cured a paralysed man almost as an afterthought to forgiving his sins (Mk 2:1-12), and frequently he restored a person's health because they had shown great faith in him (Lk 7:1-10).

Jesus also charged his apostles with the task of spreading the good news and healing the sick :

> *So they set off to preach repentance; and they cast out many devils, and anointed many sick people with oil and cured them.* (Mk 6:12-13)

This pattern continued after Jesus's death and resurrection. The early Church community saw forgiveness and healing as an important part of being faithful to Jesus's mission:

> *If any one of you is in trouble, he should pray; if anyone is feeling happy, he should sing a psalm. If one of you is ill, he should send for the elders of the church, and they must anoint him with oil in the name of the Lord and pray over him. The prayer of faith will save the sick man and the Lord will raise him up again; and if he has committed any sins, he will be*

forgiven. So confess your sins to one another, and pray for one another, and this will cure you; the heartfelt prayer of a good man works very powerfully. (James 5:13-16)

Today the Church celebrates this promise in the sacrament of the anointing of the sick. The important elements of this sacrament are the prayer of faith (by the priest, the sick person and the community), the laying on of hands which invokes the Holy Spirit, and the anointing with oil.

The proper place for celebrating this sacrament is the home parish or community of the sick person, the place where they have to address their sickness and where they are supported by other Christians in the local Church. However, in Lourdes this sacrament can often be celebrated with fellow pilgrims in such a way that this genuine communal care and continuing support is manifested.

Anointing of the sick is not reserved for people who are about to die. It is a sacrament to help us live. It is about bringing our faith in God to bear on those difficult situations, caused by sickness, which require the help of grace - grace for us to continue living fully the life we are called to as sons and daughters of God. It is about being saved and raised up.

At the same time it is not a sacrament for those minor inconveniences which can easily be dealt with by a dose of medicine or a heart to heart session of spiritual counselling. The mind of the Church is that this sacrament is for those whose health is seriously impaired by sickness or old age, and those about to undergo an important surgical operation (*Pastoral Care of the Sick*, 8-15). A sensible, unscrupulous decision is called for. If in doubt, a pilgrim should consult the chaplain, the pilgrimage director or a doctor.

Many pilgrimages in Lourdes offer the opportunity to celebrate this sacrament communally (except in cases of emergency), and often within Mass. Such services are usually designed specially for this occasion by pilgrimage liturgy directors, and broadly take the following form:

1 Introductory Rites

A hymn or song is sung as the assembly gathers and the sick are seated in the body of the church. After the sign of the cross and greeting, the presider (often a bishop with several of his priests) welcomes the sick people and the wider congregation, and, after calling on the mercy of God, says an opening prayer asking for courage and healing.

2 Liturgy of the Word

The word of God is proclaimed to the assembly. It may speak of Jesus's own ministry to the sick, and of his promise to save and raise up those who call upon his name. A psalm and gospel acclamation may be sung, and the presider preaches a homily illustrating how the word of God bears upon the meaning of illness and the grace given in the sacrament of anointing.

3 Liturgy of Anointing

There are five separate elements to the liturgy of anointing:

a) Litany

A litany, with suitable responses, is sung (or said) to invoke God's grace upon the sick and those who care for them.

b) Laying on of Hands

The presider, and any other priests, goes among the sick people and in silence lays his hands on their heads. When several priests are present they assist him in laying hands on some of the sick. This silent prayer is to call down the Holy Spirit of healing, asking that God's love be upon us as we place all our hope in him.

c) Prayer over the Oil

The oil is usually olive oil that was blessed by the bishop at the Chrism Mass. A prayer of thanksgiving is said over this oil, with suitable responses. If, however, fresh oil is to be blessed during this liturgy, the following or similar prayer may be used:

God of all consolation,
you chose and sent your Son to heal the world.
Graciously listen to our prayer of faith:
send the power of your Holy Spirit, the Consoler,
into this precious oil, this soothing ointment,
this rich gift, this fruit of the earth.
Bless this oil + and sanctify it for our use.
Make this oil a remedy for all who are anointed with it;
heal them in body, in soul, and in spirit,
and deliver them from every affliction.
We ask this through our Lord Jesus Christ, your Son,
who lives and reigns with you and the Holy Spirit,
one God, for ever and ever.
Amen.

d) Anointing

The presider and other ministers anoint with the oil those who are sick.

Anointing the forehead, he says:

Through this holy anointing
may the Lord in his love and mercy help you
with the grace of the Holy Spirit.

Amen.

Anointing the hands, he says:

May the Lord who frees you from sin
save you and raise you up.

Amen.

If there is a large number of people to be anointed, a song or psalm may now be sung.

e) Prayer after Anointing

The liturgy of anointing concludes with a prayer in which the presider prays for the sick, asking God that they may experience comfort, courage, patience, hope and support in their suffering.

4 Liturgy of the Eucharist *(If a Mass is being celebrated)*

5 Concluding Rites

At the end of the celebration the presider blesses all present with the following or similar blessing:

> May the God of all consolation
> bless you in every way
> and grant you hope all the days of your life.
> **Amen.**

> May God restore you to health
> and grant you salvation.
>
> **Amen.**

> May God fill your heart with peace
> and lead you to eternal life.
>
> **Amen.**

> May almighty God bless you,
> the Father, and the Son, +
> and the Holy Spirit.
>
> **Amen.**

The liturgy usually concludes with a dismissal and a hymn or song.

PART FOUR

"PENANCE, PENANCE, PENANCE"

Morning Prayer: Communal

Morning Prayer: Individual

Blessed Sacrament Procession

Torchlight Procession

Way of the Cross for Lourdes

Evening Prayer: Communal

Night Prayer: Individual

MORNING PRAYER : COMMUNAL

INTRODUCTION

Leader: O God, come to our aid.

All: **O Lord, make haste to help us**
Glory be to the Father and to the Son and to
the Holy Spirit, as it was in the beginning, is
now and ever shall be, world without end.
Amen. (Alleluia)

HYMN

The following hymn may be used, or another suitable hymn or song
chosen from the selection on pages 218-298.

Transcendent God in whom we live,
The Resurrection and the Light,
We sing for you a morning hymn
To end the silence of the night.

When earthly cock begins its crow
And everything from sleep awakes,
New life and hope spring up again
While out of darkness colour breaks.

Creator of all things that are,
The measure and the end of all,
Forgiving God, forget our sins,
And hear our prayer before we call.

Praise Father, Son and Holy Ghost,
Blest Trinity and source of grace,
Who call us out of nothingness
To find in you our resting-place.

Other psalms, canticles, scripture readings and prayers may be chosen.
If the antiphons are used, they are sung (or said) before and after each
psalm or canticle.

PSALMODY

Psalm 62

Antiphon I

To you, O God, I keep vigil at dawn, to look upon your power.
(Alleluia)

O God, you are my God, for your I long;
for you my soul is thirsting.
My body pines for you
like a dry, weary land without water.
So I gaze on you in the sanctuary
to see your strength and your glory.

For your love is better than life,
my lips will speak your praise.
So I will bless you all my life,
in your name I will lift up my hands.
My soul is filled as with a banquet,
my mouth shall praise you with joy.

On my bed I remember you.
On you I muse through the night
for you have been my help;
in the shadow of your wings I rejoice.
My soul clings to you;
your right hand holds me fast.

Glory be to the Father and to the Son
and to the Holy Spirit.
As it was in the beginning, is now and ever shall be,
world without end. Amen.

Antiphon I

To you, O God, I keep vigil at dawn, to look upon your power.
(Alleluia)

Canticle of Daniel (3:57-88,56)

Antiphon II

The three sang with one voice in the heart of the fire:
Blessed be God. (Alleluia)

O all you works of the Lord, O bless the Lord.
To him be highest glory and praise for ever.
And you, angels of the Lord, O bless the Lord.
To him be highest glory and praise for ever.

And you, the heavens of the Lord, O bless the Lord.
And you, clouds of the sky, O bless the Lord.
And you, all armies of the Lord, O bless the Lord.
To him be highest glory and praise for ever.

And you, sun and moon, O bless the Lord.
And you, the stars of the heav'ns, O bless the Lord.
And you, showers and rain, O bless the Lord.
To him be highest glory and praise for ever.

And you, all you breezes and winds, O bless the Lord.
And you, fire and heat, O bless the Lord.
And you, cold and heat, O bless the Lord.
To him be highest glory and praise for ever.

And you, showers and dew, O bless the Lord.
And you, frosts and cold, O bless the Lord.
And you, frost and snow, O bless the Lord.
To him be highest glory and praise for ever.

And you, night-time and day, O bless the Lord.
And you, darkness and light, O bless the Lord.
And you, lightning and clouds, O bless the Lord.
To him be highest glory and praise for ever.

O let the earth bless the Lord.
To him be highest glory and praise for ever.

And you, mountains and hills, O bless the Lord.
And you, all plants of the earth, O bless the Lord.
And you, fountains and springs, O bless the Lord.
To him be highest glory and praise for ever.

And you, rivers and seas, O bless the Lord.
And you, creatures of the sea, O bless the Lord.
And you, every bird in the sky, O bless the Lord.
And you, wild beasts and tame, O bless the Lord.
To him be highest glory and praise for ever.

And you, children of men, O bless the Lord.
To him be highest glory and praise for ever.

O Israel, bless the Lord, O bless the Lord.
And you, princes of the Lord, O bless the Lord.
And you, servants of the Lord, O bless the Lord.
To him be highest glory and praise for ever.

And you, spirits and souls of the just, O bless the Lord.
And you, holy and humble of heart, O bless the Lord.
Ananias, Azarias, Mizael, O bless the Lord.
To him be highest glory and praise for ever.

Let us praise the Father, the Son, and the Holy Spirit:
To you be highest glory and praise for ever.
May you be blessed, O Lord, in the heavens.
To you be highest glory and praise for ever.

Antiphon II

The three sang with one voice in the heart of the fire:
Blessed be God. (Alleluia)

Psalm 149

Antiphon III

Let Sion's sons exult in their king. (Alleluia)

Sing a new song to the Lord,
his praise in the assembly of the faithful.
Let Israel rejoice in its Maker,
let Sion's sons exult in their king.
Let them praise his name with dancing
and make music with the timbrel and harp.

For the Lord takes delight in his people.
He crowns the poor with salvation.
Let the faithful rejoice in their glory,
shout for joy and take their rest.
Let the praise of God be on their lips
and a two-edged sword in their hand,

to deal out vengeance to the nations
and punishment on all the peoples;
to bind their kings in chains
and their nobles in fetters of iron;
to carry out the sentence pre-ordained:
this honour is for all his faithful.

Glory be to the Father and to the Son
and to the Holy Spirit,
As it was in the beginning, is now and ever shall be,
world without end. Amen.

Antiphon III

Let Sion's sons exult in their king. (Alleluia)

SCRIPTURE READING   (*Revelation* 7:10,12)

Victory to our God, who sits on the throne, and to the Lamb!
Praise and glory and wisdom and thanksgiving and honour
and power and strength to our God for ever and ever. Amen.

SHORT RESPONSORY

Leader: You are the Christ, the Son of the living God. Have
mercy on us.
All: **You are the Christ, the Son of the living God.
Have mercy on us.**
Leader: You are seated at the right hand of the Father.
All: **Have mercy on us.**
Leader: Glory be to the Father and to the Son and to the
Holy Spirit.
All: **You are the Christ, the Son of the living God.
Have mercy on us.**

CANTICLE OF ZECHARIAH (Benedictus) (*Luke* 1:68-79)

Antiphon

The greatest among you must be your servant, says the Lord.

Blessed be the Lord, the God of Israel!
He has visited his people and redeemed them.

He has raised up for us a mighty saviour
in the house of David his servant,
as he promised by the lips of holy men,
those who were his prophets from of old.

A saviour who would free us from our foes,
from the hands of all who hate us.
So his love for our fathers is fulfiled
and his holy covenant remembered.

He swore to Abraham our father to grant us,
that free from fear, and saved from the hands of our foes,
we might serve him in holiness and justice
all the days of our lives in his presence.

As for you, little child,
you shall be called a prophet of God, the Most High.
You shall go ahead of the Lord
to prepare his ways before him,

To make known to his people their salvation
through forgiveness of all their sins,
the loving-kindness of the heart of our God
who visits us like the dawn from on high.

He will give light to those in darkness,
those who dwell in the shadow of death,
and guide us into the way of peace.

Glory be to the Father and to the Son
and to the Holy Spirit.
As it was in the beginning, is now and ever shall be,
world without end. Amen.

Antiphon

The greatest among you must be your servant, says the Lord.

INTERCESSIONS

Leader: As this new day begins, we pray to Christ our Lord who is the Morning Star which gives light to all peoples:

All: **Lord Jesus, give light to our hearts and minds**

Leader: Give us the grace to serve you during this day:

All: **Lord Jesus, give light to our hearts and minds**

Leader: May our eyes be open to the needs of those we meet:

All: **Lord Jesus, give light to our hearts and minds**

Leader: Bring comfort to the sick and the dying:

All: **Lord Jesus, give light to our hearts and minds**

Leader: Take away our pride, temper our anger and teach us forgiveness:

All: **Lord Jesus, give light to our hearts and minds**

Leader: May all men and women come to know you as Lord:

All: **Lord Jesus, give light to our hearts and minds**

Pause for any other intentions...

All: **Our Father...**

Leader: Lord of the morning,
increase in us your gift of faith,
so that all our actions may begin from you,
and in you find their true completion,
through Christ our Lord.

All: **Amen**

CONCLUSION

Leader: May almighty God bless us,
the Father, and the Son,
and the Holy Spirit.

All: **Amen.**

Leader: Let us bless the Lord.

All: **Thanks be to God.**

MORNING PRAYER : INDIVIDUAL

The following form of Morning Prayer offers a simple pattern that can be used or adapted by an individual at any time of the year. For the fuller communal celebration of Morning Prayer (Lauds), based on the Divine Office of the Church, see pages 141-147

SIGN OF THE CROSS AND PRAISE OF GOD

In the name of the Father,
and of the Son,
and of the Holy Spirit. Amen.

I will praise you, my God
and bless your name for ever.
Every day I will call on you
and bless your name for ever.

Great is the Lord
and worthy of all praise.
I will declare your greatness, Lord,
and bless your name for ever.

Glory be to the Father,
and to the Son,
and to the Holy Spirit;
as it was in the beginning,
is now, and ever shall be,
world without end. Amen.

GOD'S WORD   (*Lamentations* 3:22-26)

The steadfast love of the Lord never ceases,
his mercies never come to an end;
they are new every morning;
great is your faithfulness.
"The Lord is my portion," says my soul,
"therefore I will hope in him."
The Lord is good to those who wait for him,

to the soul that seeks him.
It is good that one should wait quietly
for the salvation of the Lord.

(Pause for reflection)

PRAYERS

Morning Offering

Loving God, I thank you for giving me life
and for bringing me safely to this new day.
Be with me as I go about my daily tasks.
I offer you today all my thoughts,
words and actions for your service.
Use me to bring your healing touch,
your smile of friendship,
your word of encouragement,
and your helping hand,
for the sake of Jesus Christ our Lord.
Amen.

Act of Trust

Lord, without you I am nothing,
but with your grace I can accomplish much.
I depend on you for help.
Stay with me when I come close to temptation;
stand before me when I feel weary,
and be at my side
when great things are asked of me.
Walk with me and let me feel your presence
when I need you most,
for you are Lord, for ever and ever.
Amen.

Intercessions and Lord's Prayer

Father of all, I pray to you
for those whom I will meet during this day,
and especially for...

I pray for my family and friends,
those with whom I work
and those who rely on me…

I pray for those in need:
for the sick, the lonely,
and for those who feel unloved…

I pray for those who are seeking work,
those with no roof over their heads,
and those who are forced to be refugees…

I pray for those who are in government,
those who make and dispense laws,
and those who serve our public needs…

As I pray for your world,
and for all that is dear to you,
I join my prayers with those of your saints,
and in the words of your Son I call upon you:

Our Father,…

CONCLUSION

Lord of the morning,
I bless you for being my God.
In your goodness,
return your blessing upon me
during this new day which you have made,
that I may serve you as you deserve,
and come to know your mercy.
May I heed the promptings of your Spirit,
recognize your Son in those I meet,
and be a witness to your glory
today and evermore.
I ask you this through Christ our Lord.
Amen.

BLESSED SACRAMENT PROCESSION

Each afternoon at 4.30pm the Blessed Sacrament Procession is held. People begin to line up about half an hour earlier starting outside the Bernadette Centre on the opposite side of the river to the Grotto. If you are with a pilgrimage and are walking with a diocese or other organization, remember to check the time and place of your rendez-vous. When rain or excessive heat intervene, a celebration of prayer and adoration takes place in the Underground Basilica and starts at the same time.)

The procession moves off through the Domaine and passes the Crowned Statue, moving by the side of the old Accueil Notre Dame and towards St Michael's Gate. It turns at the gate and makes its way back to the Rosary Square. When all have returned, the priest or bishop carrying the Blessed Sacrament blesses first the sick and handicapped, before mounting the steps of the Rosary Basilica where Benediction takes place.

For Christians the Eucharist is the centre of our faith. We are never more Church than when together we are eating and drinking the Body and Blood of Christ. That sacramental presence of Jesus abides under the form of bread and wine, and when we take part in the procession we are professing our faith in the reality of Christ's presence among us. To walk in the procession is to acknowledge our need of the Bread of Life, to thank Jesus for the gift of his very self, and to pray for all in our world which is starved of the food from heaven. It is a time of listening to God's word, a time of adoration, a time of prayer and a time of blessing.

During the procession there are meditations, prayers, hymns and chants. We are invited to respond with acclamations to invocations to Jesus based upon scripture. Some of these are spoken (in several different languages), while others are sung. The leader will announce the spoken acclamations; among the sung responses which may be used are the following:

LAUDA SION

Lauda Sion Salvatorem,
Lauda ducem et pastorem,
In hymnis et canticis.

(*Sion praise your Saviour,*
Praise your guide and your shepherd,
With hymns and songs)

BENEDICTUS QUI VENIT

Benedictus qui venit, in nomine Domini.[x2]
Hosanna, Hosanna, Hosanna in excelsis.

(*Blessed is he who comes, in the name of the Lord.[x2]*
Hosanna, Hosanna, Hosanna in the highest.)

LAUDA JERUSALEM

Lauda Jerusalem Dominum,
Lauda Deum tuum Sion.
Hosanna, Hosanna,
Hosanna Filio David.

(*Jerusalem praise your Lord,*
Praise your God, O Sion.
Hosanna, Hosanna,
Hosanna to the Son of David.)

O SALUTARIS HOSTIA

O Salutaris hostia,
Quae caeli pandis ostium,
Bella premunt hostilia,
Da robur, fer auxilium.

Uni Trinoque Domino
Sit sempiterna gloria,
Qui vitam sine termino
Nobis donet in patria. Amen.

(*O saving victim, opening wide,*
The gate of heav'n to man below;
Our foes press on from every side;
Thine aid supply, thy strength bestow.

To thy great name be endless praise,
Immortal Godhead, one in three;
O grant us endless length of days
In our true native land with thee. Amen.)

TANTUM ERGO

Tantum ergo sacramentum
Veneremur cernui:
Et antiquum documentum
Novo cedat ritui;
Praestat fides supplementum
Sensuum defectui.

Genitori, genitoque
Laus et jubilatio,
Salus, honor, virtus quoque
Sit et benedictio;
Procedenti ab utroque
Compar sit laudatio. Amen.

(Therefore we, before him bending,
This great sacrament revere;
Types and shadows have their ending,
For the newer rite is here;
Faith, our outward sense befriending,
Makes the inward vision clear.

Glory let us give and blessing
To the Father and the Son,
Honour, might, and praise addressing,
While eternal ages run;
Ever too his love confessing
Who from both, with both is one. Amen.)

When the Blessed Sacrament procession is over, pilgrims
are asked to keep the SILENCE which should be observed at
all times in the Domaine. This allows those who wish to
continue in prayer to remain undisturbed by unnecessary
noise.

THE TORCHLIGHT PROCESSION

At 8.45pm each evening a Marian Celebration and Torchlight Procession begins from near the Grotto, and rather like the Blessed Sacrament Procession, it passes the statue of the Crowned Virgin, proceeds towards the St Michael's Gate and returns on itself to finish in Rosary Square.

It takes its name from the fact that pilgrims, usually walking behind their diocesan banner, carry candles in the procession, which thereby takes on the picturesque aspect of a blaze of light snaking its way through the processional route towards the Rosary Basilica, which near the end of the ceremony is illuminated. This effect is heightened by the custom of raising the candles in the air at certain points of the ceremony. These candles can be bought, along with a small holder which contains the words to some of the songs, from almost any of the many shops in Lourdes. Make sure you buy a candle-holder with the language you require.

During the procession five decades of the Rosary are recited. Often the Our Father is said in Latin, the ten Hail Marys are said in as many different languages (the first half being spoken over the public address by a single voice or small group), and the Glory Be is then sung by everyone in Latin.

Of course, it does not matter which language you use to reply, since the Domaine will be filled with thousands of pilgrims each praying in a different language. The real purpose of the procession is to honour Mary with our songs and prayers, and to recall our baptismal commitment to keep the Light of Christ burning brightly in our lives. By so doing, we give praise to the God who has called us out of darkness into glorious light.

Among the prayers and songs used during the Torchlight Procession, given here in Latin and French where useful, are the following:

THE MYSTERIES OF THE ROSARY

The Joyful Mysteries

1 The Annunciation

2 The Visitation

3 The Nativity

4 The Presentation in the Temple

5 The Finding of the Child Jesus in the Temple

The Sorrowful Mysteries

1 The Agony in the Garden

2 The Scourging at the Pillar

3 The Crowning with Thorns

4 The Carrying of the Cross

5 The Crucifixion

The Glorious Mysteries

1 The Resurrection

2 The Ascension

3 The Descent of the Holy Spirit

4 The Assumption

5 The Crowning of the Blessed Virgin Mary

OUR FATHER

Our Father, who art in heaven,
hallowed be thy name.
Thy kingdom come.
Thy will be done on earth,
as it is in heaven.
Give us this day our daily bread,
and forgive us our trespasses,
as we forgive those who trespass against us,
and lead us not into temptation,
but deliver us from evil. Amen,

(Latin)

Pater noster, qui es in caelis:
sanctificetur nomen tuum;
adveniat regnum tuum;
fiat voluntas tua, sicut in caelo et in terra.
Panem nostrum cotidianum da nobis hodie;
et dimitte nobis debita nostra,
sicut et nos dimittimus debitoribus nostris;
et ne nos inducas in tentationem;
sed libera nos a malo. Amen.

(French)

Notre Père, qui es aux cieux,
que ton nom soit sanctifié,
que ton règne vienne,
que ta volonté soit faite
sur la terre comme au ciel.
Donne-nous aujourd'hui
notre pain de ce jour.
Pardonne-nous nos offenses,
comme nous pardonnons aussi
à ceux qui nous ont offensés,
et ne nous soumets pas à la tentation,
mais délivre-nous du Mal. Amen.

HAIL MARY

Hail Mary, full of grace,
the Lord is with thee.
Blessed art thou among women,
and blessed is the fruit of thy womb, Jesus;
Holy Mary, mother of God,
pray for us sinners,
now and at the hour of our death. Amen.

(Latin)

Ave Maria, gratia plena,
Dominus tecum.
Benedicta tu in mulieribus,
et benedictus fructus ventris tui, Jesus;
Sancta Maria, mater Dei,
ora pro nobis peccatoribus,
nunc et in hora mortis nostrae. Amen.

(French)

Je vous salue Marie, pleine de grâce,
le Seigneur est avec vous.
Vous êtes bénie entre toutes les femmes,
et Jésus, le fruit de vos entrailles, est béni.
Sainte Marie, mère de Dieu,
priez pour nous, pauvres pécheurs,
maintenant et à l'heure de notre mort. Amen.

GLORY BE TO THE FATHER

Glory be to the Father, and to the Son,
and to the Holy Spirit;
as it was in the beginning,
is now and ever shall be
world without end. Amen.

(Latin)

Gloria Patri, et Filio,
et Spiritui Sancto;
sicut erat in principio,

et nunc et semper
et in saecula saeculorum. Amen.

(French)

Gloire au Père, et au Fils,
et au Saint-Esprit;
comme il était au commencement,
et maintenant et toujours
dans tous les siècles des siècles. Amen.

LOURDES HYMN

The Lourdes hymn is sung as the procession winds its way to Rosary Square:

1   O Mary, our mother,
    We come to this place
    where you, who are sinless,
    Appeared full of grace.

> *Ave, Ave, Ave Maria,*
> *Ave, Ave, Ave Maria.*

2   As Bernadette waited
    There came to her sight
    A radiant Lady,
    Surrounded by light.

3   She gave her a message:
    "Let penance be done,
    And pray that all sinners
    May turn to my Son.

4   Come here in procession,
    To praise God and sing,
    To wash in these waters
    And drink at this spring."

5   She asked that a chapel
    Be built in this place;
    That all be encouraged
    To pray for God's grace.

6 The Lady responded
  When asked for her name:
  "Conceived without sin
  Is the title I claim."

7 O mother of mercy,
  Our sorrows relieve;
  Sustain those who suffer;
  Console those who grieve.

8 O bless us, dear Lady,
  With blessings from heaven;
  And to our petitions
  let answer be given.

As everyone reaches the Square, some intercessions are sung with the following refrain:

LAUDATE MARIAM

Laudate, laudate, laudate Mariam,
Laudate, laudate, laudate Mariam!

(*Praise, praise, praise Mary!*)

FINAL BLESSING

The bishops and priests present invoke God's blessing:

  Sit nomen Domini benedictum

All: **Ex hoc nunc et usque in saeculum**

  Adjutorium nostrum in nomine Domini

All: **Qui fecit caelum et terram**

  Benedicat vos omnipotens Deus,
  Pater, + et Filius, et Spiritus Sanctus.

All: **Amen**

The Torchlight Procession concludes with the singing of the Hail Holy Queen (Salve Regina)

SALVE REGINA

Salve Regina, Mater misericordiae,
Vita, dulcedo et spes nostra, salve.
Ad te clamamus, exsules filii Hevae.
Ad te suspiramus, gementes et flentes
In hac lacrimarum valle.
Eia ergo, Advocata nostra,
Illos tuos misericordes oculos
Ad nos converte.
Et Jesum, benedictum fructum ventris tui,
Nobis post hoc exsilium ostende.
O clemens, O pia, O dulcis Virgo Maria.

The usual request for TOTAL SILENCE applies after the Torchlight Procession. Many pilgrims use this opportunity to pay a final visit to the Grotto before returning to their hotels.

WAY OF THE CROSS FOR LOURDES

The Passion of Jesus has been for long at the centre of Christian devotion. By meditating on the path he took to his suffering and death, we remind ourselves of the sacrifice he made on our behalf, and of our need to imitate him in our own Christian lives.

Today the Way of the Cross is followed in many fashions. Some people are able to travel along the Via Dolorosa on the streets of Jerusalem, retracing what are the very footsteps of Jesus. Others follow the Stations (stopping points) by walking around a church, while some prefer to make them at home.

In Lourdes the Stations are arranged so that all can take part in them, pilgrims who are able-bodied and those who have difficulty in getting about. Details of the locations are to be found on p.46.

Traditionally there have been fourteen Stations based loosely upon the gospel accounts of the Passion, and supplemented with a few devotional scenes. In recent years an extra Station has often been added to commemorate the resurrection, which completes the whole picture of the events of that first Holy Week. The heart of Christ's saving work for us, the Paschal Mystery, is not just his death but also his resurrection. He gave himself up to death on Calvary, but he triumphed over death by rising from the dead and thereby offering us the chance of new life.

In addition to this extra Station, there is a further one which is used in one of the Ways of the Cross in Lourdes, though it is not found in other places and therefore is not normally included in any list of the Stations. As part of the lower Stations (for the sick, on the flat and near the river bank), the fifteenth Station recalls the hope and faith of Mary as she awaited the third day. The resurrection then becomes the sixteenth Station.

The following Way of the Cross is designed specifically for use in Lourdes.

1 ST STATION

Jesus is condemned to death

Leader: We adore you, O Christ, and we praise you.

All: **Because by your holy cross you have redeemed the world.**

Reader: *So when Pilate saw that he could do nothing, but rather that a riot was beginning, he took some water and washed his hands before the crowd, saying,"I am innocent of this man's blood; see to it yourselves." Then the people as a whole answered, "His blood be on us and on our children!" So he released Barabbas for them; and after flogging Jesus, he handed him over to be crucified.* (Matthew 27:24-26)

(Pause for reflection)

Leader: Pilate lives in each of us. We know what it is to wash our hands of problems we find too difficult to cope with. Do we take the hard decisions or do we court popularity? Wherever there is suffering and injustice, we cannot remain outsiders or uninvolved.

Prayer: *Lord of justice and truth, give us the courage to stand up for what we know to be right. When we are tempted to look the other way, to go with the crowd, give us the strength of your Spirit that we may be proud to profess our faith in your Son.*

Leader: For those who are falsely accused, those whose reputations are unjustly destroyed, and those who suffer imprisonment for crimes they did not commit:

Lord, in your mercy (sung)

All: **Hear our prayer (*sung*)**

All: **I love you, Jesus my love, above all things; I repent with my whole heart for having offended you. Never permit me to separate myself from you again. Grant that I may love you always and then do with me what you will.**

2 ND STATION

Jesus takes up his cross

Leader: We adore you, O Christ, and we praise you.

All: **Because by your holy cross you have redeemed the world.**

Reader: *So they took Jesus; and carrying the cross by himself, he went out to what is called The Place of the Skull, which in Hebrew is called Golgotha.(John 19:16-17)*

(Pause for reflection)

Leader: What have we done to our God? Bruised, lacerated and bleeding he accepts for us the tree that would bring both torment and victory. Bearing our own particular cross - of sickness, tiredness, grief - is the way God invites us to triumph over sin and evil.

Prayer: *God of eternal hope, you promise us an easy yoke and a burden which is light. Sustain us under the weight of our sufferings, under the strain of our responsibilities, under the stress of our daily routine. Stand by our side and stay close to us.*

Leader: For those who have just been diagnosed with terminal illness, those whose pain is increasing, and those who are the victims of violence:

Lord, in your mercy *(sung)*

All: **Hear our prayer** *(sung)*

All **I love you, Jesus my love, above all things; I repent with my whole heart for having offended you. Never permit me to separate myself from you again. Grant that I may love you always and then do with me what you will.**

3 RD STATION

Jesus falls the first time

Leader: We adore you, O Christ, and we praise you.

All: **Because by your holy cross you have redeemed the world.**

Reader: *Surely he has borne our infirmities and carried our diseases; yet we accounted him stricken, struck down by God, and afflicted. But he was wounded for our transgressions, crushed for our iniquities; upon him was the punishment that made us whole, and by his bruises we are healed.*(Isaiah 53:4-5)

(Pause for reflection)

Leader: If only for a moment, it seems as if God has been cut down to our size, as under the weight of the cross Jesus falls to the ground. It appears as if all his work on earth is about to be undone: his teaching, his miracles, his reason for becoming one of us. This he accepts, knowing that to do the will of the Father can only lead to glory.

Prayer: *God of patient endurance, lift us up when we are low. When we fall at the feet of despair, when sickness drags us down, and when we are toppled by our pride, save us and raise us up.*

Leader: For those who suffer from depression, those who have lost hope, and those who feel the burden of tending for a loved-one who is sick:

Lord, in your mercy *(sung)*

All: **Hear our prayer** *(sung)*

All: I love you, Jesus my love, above all things; I repent with my whole heart for having offended you. Never permit me to separate myself from you again. Grant that I may love you always and then do with me what you will.

4TH STATION

Jesus meets his mother Mary

Leader: We adore you, O Christ, and we praise you.

All: **Because by your holy cross you have redeemed the world.**

Reader: *Then Simeon blessed them and said to his mother Mary, "This child is destined for the falling and rising of many in Israel, and to be a sign that will be opposed so that the inner thoughts of many will be revealed - and a sword will pierce your own soul too."(Luke 2.34-35)*

(Pause for reflection)

Leader: Mary too shares the suffering of her son. The cross is laid upon her shoulders, the fingers of blame point at her. Yet her trust in God is constant: Let what you have said be done to me. Christ's passion is the source of our compassion; we are called to share the suffering of others.

Prayer: *God of tenderness and compassion, be close to those who cry tears of pain. Encourage those who weep for their own sinfulness, that their sorrow may be turned into tears of joy.*

Leader: For mothers whose children are sick, for parents whose children have gone missing, and for families who suffer public humiliation:

Lord, in your mercy *(sung)*

All: **Hear our prayer *(sung)***

All: **I love you, Jesus my love, above all things; I repent with my whole heart for having offended you. Never permit me to separate myself from you again. Grant that I may love you always and then do with me what you will.**

5TH STATION

Simon of Cyrene carries the cross

Leader: We adore you, O Christ, and we praise you.

All: **Because by your holy cross you have redeemed the world.**

Reader: *As they led him away, they seized a man, Simon of Cyrene, who was coming form the country, and they laid the cross on him, and made him carry it behind Jesus. (Luke 23:26)*

(Pause for reflection)

Leader: Although Simon was forced to carry Jesus's cross, there are many here in Lourdes who willingly help us on our pilgrimage. We in turn are invited to that generosity of spirit which does not look idly on, but grows through its service of others.

Prayer: *Ever-present Lord, help us to be your hands, your feet and your shoulders as we serve those here in need. May we speak your words of kindness and listen with attentiveness to those who claim our time.*

Leader: For those who have helped us on our pilgrimage, those who have looked after our travel and accommodation, for the Lourdes Hospitality and for those who prepare and lead our acts of worship:

Lord, in your mercy *(sung)*

All: **Hear our prayer *(sung)***

All: **I love you, Jesus my love, above all things; I repent with my whole heart for having offended you. Never permit me to separate myself from you again. Grant that I may love you always and then do with me what you will.**

6TH STATION

Veronica wipes the face of Jesus

Leader: We adore you, O Christ, and we praise you.

All: **Because by your holy cross you have redeemed the world.**

Reader: *He had no form or majesty that we should look at him, nothing in his appearance that we should desire him. He was despised and rejected by others; a man of suffering and acquainted with infirmity; and as one from whom others hide their faces he was despised, and we held him of no account. (Isaiah 53:2-3)*

(Pause for reflection)

Leader: Ancient tradition tells us that the face of Jesus, the image of the unseen God, was left on the cloth which Veronica used when she met Jesus. We too can see that same face in every act of kindness, every offer of support, and every work of mercy that is done for the sake of Christ Jesus.

Prayer: *God, hidden from our eyes, imprint your likeness upon our hearts. Help us to recognize you in the faces of those who are despised, marginalized and unloved. May we bring the light of your face to those in need.*

Leader: For those whose bodies have been mutilated in wars, those who have been paralysed during violent conflict, and those who suffer from malnutrition:

Lord, in your mercy *(sung)*

All: **Hear our prayer** *(sung)*

All: **I love you, Jesus my love, above all things; I repent with my whole heart for having offended you. Never permit me to separate myself from you again. Grant that I may love you always and then do with me what you will.**

7TH STATION

Jesus falls the second time

Leader: We adore you, O Christ, and we praise you.

All: **Because by your holy cross you have redeemed the world.**

Reader: *Now that I have fallen, they gather around delighted. They crowd about to jeer at me. They take me by surprise, strike me and tear me to pieces. They provoke me with their mockery and their jibes, as they gnash their teeth at me. (Psalm 34:15-16)*

(Pause for reflection)

Leader: Continually falling and getting up again is the story of our sinful journey to God. Jesus, who was sinless and innocent, also had to make that effort to stand up once more and continue his journey to the cross. No matter how many times we fall, each time we arise we will encounter the mercy of God.

Prayer: *Lord of the journey, you know how deeply we fall and how often we become discouraged by our own obstinacy and short-sightedness. Be with us on our pilgrimage of life, reach out to catch us, and raise us up in the warmth of your loving embrace.*

Leader: For those who have suffered a relapse in their sickness, for those enjoying a period of remission and for those who are finding it hard to keep going:

Lord, in your mercy (*sung*)

All: **Hear our prayer (*sung*)**

All: **I love you, Jesus my love, above all things; I repent with my whole heart for having offended you. Never permit me to separate myself from you again. Grant that I may love you always and then do with me what you will.**

8TH STATION

Jesus meets the women of Jerusalem

Leader: We adore you, O Christ, and we praise you.

All: **Because by your holy cross you have redeemed the world.**

Reader: *A great number of the people followed him, and among them were women who were beating their breasts and wailing for him. But Jesus turned to them and said, "Daughters of Jerusalem, do not weep for me, but weep for yourselves and for your children." (Luke 23:27-28)*

(Pause for reflection)

Leader: From the midst of his pain and anguish Jesus holds out hope to the women of Jerusalem. Yet he warns them not merely to lament the awful spectacle, but to look deeply at the paradox of what is really happening, to realize what this means for posterity. We are the children of those women, and Jesus's call to repentance is made to us today.

Prayer: *God of all truth, we acknowledge our sins and our faults are always before us. Give us the grace to see those ways which lead us into darkness, and grant us the wisdom to turn our steps towards your light.*

Leader: For those preparing for the sacrament of reconciliation, those who take the blame for the faults of others, and those who fail to speak in the defence of the innocent:

Lord, in your mercy (*sung*)

All: **Hear our prayer (*sung*)**

All: **I love you, Jesus my love, above all things; I repent with my whole heart for having offended you. Never permit me to separate myself from you again. Grant that I may love you always and then do with me what you will.**

9TH STATION

Jesus falls the third time

Leader: We adore you, O Christ, and we praise you.

All: **Because by your holy cross you have redeemed the world.**

Reader: *Christ Jesus, though he was in the form of God, did not regard equality with God as something to be exploited, but emptied himself, taking the form of a slave, being born in human likeness. And being found in human form, he humbled himself and became obedient to the point of death - even death on a cross. (Philippians 2:6-8)*

(Pause for reflection)

Leader: The indignity for Jesus of falling for the third time is matched only by our frequent falling away from him. He freely chose the path of obedience and self-denial. We fall from him by our half-hearted following of the gospel, by our half-kept promises of fidelity and by putting our own comfort before our Christian duty.

Prayer: *Lord of the new and everlasting covenant, by our sins we have denied you three times and more. When we fall short of your calling, raise us up and give us the grace to put all our strength at the service of your will, that by being humbled we may be exalted in your glory.*

Leader: For those who have fallen into a coma, those who suffer from chronic and painful illness, and for all physicians, surgeons and nurses:

Lord, in your mercy (*sung*)

All: **Hear our prayer (*sung*)**

All: I love you, Jesus my love, above all things; I repent with my whole heart for having offended you. Never permit me to separate myself from you again. Grant that I may love you always and then do with me what you will.

10TH STATION

Jesus is stripped of his garments

Leader: We adore you, O Christ, and we praise you.

All: **Because by your holy cross you have redeemed the world.**

Reader: *Then the soldiers of the governor took Jesus into the governor's headquarters, and they gathered the whole cohort around him. They stripped him and put a scarlet robe on him, and after twisting some thorns into a crown, they put it on his head. They put a reed in his right hand and knelt before him and mocked him, saying, "Hail, King of the Jews!" (Matthew 27:27-29)*

(Pause for reflection)

Leader: Jesus is stripped of his right to life and of his right to belong. Abandoned by those who were close to him, he stands naked, mocked and open to the gaze of those who would scorn him. Our challenge is to be stripped of all that comes between us and God, to let go of our unhealthy attachments, our prejudice and our pretensions.

Prayer: *God of every good thing, naked we came from our mother's womb, and naked shall we return to you. Help us to rid ourselves of what displeases you. Keep us firm in your love, and give us a heart that is open to the needs of our brothers and sisters.*

Leader: For those who are shunned in their sickness, for the victims of AIDS, for those with leprosy, and for those with mental illnesses:

Lord, in your mercy (*sung*)

All: **Hear our prayer (*sung*)**

All: I love you, Jesus my love, above all things; I repent with my whole heart for having offended you. Never permit me to separate myself from you again. Grant that I may love you always and then do with me what you will.

11 TH STATION

Jesus is nailed to the cross

Leader: We adore you, O Christ, and we praise you.

All: **Because by your holy cross you have redeemed the world.**

Reader: *Two others also, who were criminals, were led away to be put to death with Jesus. When they came to the place that is called The Skull, they crucified Jesus there with the criminals, one on his right and one on his left. Then Jesus said, "Father, forgive them; for they do not know what they are doing." (Luke 23:32-34)*

(Pause for reflection)

Leader: As the pain of the nails shot through his body, Jesus could have chosen to come down from the cross. Instead he chose to die among criminals, not to react to those who taunted him, and to ask his Father to forgive all who were implicated in this sorry spectacle. We can claim that forgiveness only if we do not withhold it ourselves from others.

Prayer: *Lord of the weak, protector of the vulnerable, no sin of ours can blot out your mercy. Grant that we may know our need of forgiveness, and as you stretch out your loving hand towards us, give us generosity to embrace in turn those who have done wrong to us.*

Leader: For those in dispute over medical mal-practice, for patients who have been abused, and for all who find it hard to forgive:

Lord, in your mercy *(sung)*

All: **Hear our prayer** *(sung)*

All: **I love you, Jesus my love, above all things; I repent with my whole heart for having offended you. Never permit me to separate myself from you again. Grant that I may love you always and then do with me what you will.**

12TH STATION

Jesus dies on the cross

Leader: We adore you, O Christ, and we praise you.

All: **Because by your holy cross you have redeemed the world.**

Reader: *When it was noon, darkness came over the whole land until three in the afternoon. At three o'clock Jesus cried out with a loud voice, "Eloi, Eloi, lama sabachthani?" which means, "My God, my God, why have you forsaken me?" When some of the bystanders heard it, they said, "Listen, he is calling for Elijah." And someone ran, filled a sponge with sour wine, put it on a stick, and gave it to him to drink, saying, "Wait, let us see whether Elijah will come to take him down." Then Jesus gave a loud cry and breathed his last. (Mark 15:33-37)*

(Pause for reflection)

Leader: Nailed to a tree, tormented by pain and racked with anguish, Jesus gives himself up to death. Arms outstretched, pinned down and immobile, he has been faithful to the end. Jesus has taken upon himself our sins and our sickness, and has transformed them by the victory of his death. In this act of obedience we see unfold the mystery of our redemption.

Prayer: *God of the living and the dead, in death your Son put an end to the hold of sin and sickness. Now nothing can separate us from your everlasting love. Help us to die to our old selves, that we may live the life of your Spirit, who makes of us a new creation for the glory of your name.*

Leader: For those who are in their last agony, those who will die today, and those who are afraid to die:

Lord, in your mercy *(sung)*

All: **Hear our prayer** *(sung)*

All: I love you, Jesus my love, above all things; I repent with my whole heart for having offended you. Never permit me to separate myself from you again. Grant that I may love you always and then do with me what you will.

13TH STATION

Jesus is taken down from the cross

Leader: We adore you, O Christ, and we praise you.

All: **Because by your holy cross you have redeemed the world.**

Reader: *After these things, Joseph of Arimathea, who was a disciple of Jesus, though a secret one because of his fear of the Jews, asked Pilate to let him take away the body of Jesus. Pilate gave him permission; so he came and removed the body. Nicodemus, who had at first come to Jesus by night, also came, bringing a mixture of of myrrh and aloes, weighing about a hundred pounds. (John 19:38-39)*

(Pause for reflection)

Leader: Once again Jesus is cradled in human arms as on that first night in the stable at Bethlehem. Yet it was with bewilderment that his mother and friends received his lifeless body. The question "Why did this have to happen?" is as real for them as for us today. Suffering, death and disaster are not created by God. They are permitted only as part of the mystery of eternal life, a life we enter by dying with Christ.

Prayer: *God of those who mourn, be our guide when we are lost, our light in times of darkness. When tragedy overwhelms us, when death seems senseless and grief leaves us empty, sustain our belief that by dying Jesus has destroyed our death, and is the only meaning to our lives.*

Leader: For parents who experience the death of a child, for those whose grief seems inconsolable, and those who work to support and counsel the bereaved:

Lord, in your mercy *(sung)*

All: **Hear our prayer *(sung)***

All: **I love you, Jesus my love, above all things; I repent with my whole heart for having offended you. Never permit me to separate myself from you again. Grant that I may love you always and then do with me what you will.**

14TH STATION

Jesus is laid in the tomb

Leader: We adore you, O Christ, and we praise you.

All: **Because by your holy cross you have redeemed the world.**

Reader: *Joseph of Arimathea bought a linen cloth, and taking down the body, wrapped it in the linen cloth, and laid it in a tomb that had been hewn out of the rock. He then rolled a stone against the door of the tomb. Mary Magdalene and Mary the mother of Joses saw where the body was laid.* (Mark 15:46-47)

(Pause for reflection)

Leader: The chilling silence of the tomb gives death a momentary air of victory. But death is about to lose its sting as Christ's will emerge triumphant. He has fulfiled the plan formed long ago, and his obedience and patient endurance give meaning to our daily struggles. We will not remain buried for ever under the weight of all that lays us low. Christ has set us free.

Prayer: *Ever-watchful God, be our sure hope in times of doubt, an open hand in moments of mistrust, and our constant goal when all seems lost. As we contemplate Christ's tomb, help us so to bear our cross that we may rise above what seeks to drag us down.*

Leader: For those whose illness renders them unable to communicate, for handmaids and brancardiers who give their time to us, and for those who support us at home:

Lord, in your mercy *(sung)*

All: **Hear our prayer *(sung)***

All: I love you, Jesus my love, above all things; I repent with my whole heart for having offended you. Never permit me to separate myself from you again. Grant that I may love you always and then do with me what you will.

WAY OF THE CROSS

15TH STATION

Jesus is risen from the dead

Leader: We adore you, O Christ, and we praise you.

All: **Because by your holy cross you have redeemed the world.**

Reader: *They came to the tomb and found the stone rolled away, but when they went in, they did not find the body. While they were perplexed about this, suddenly two men in dazzling clothes stood beside them. The women were terrified and bowed their faces to the ground, but the men said to them, "Why do you look for the living among the dead? He is not here, but has risen." (Lk 24:1-5)*

(Pause for reflection)

Leader: The tomb could not hold Jesus who is Lord of life. No sin, no sickness, no power can ultimately hold sway over us, now that Jesus has risen from the dead. Even death has been conquered in the power of God's Spirit. This day was made by the Lord, let us rejoice and be glad!

Prayer: *God ever new, Lord of the living, we thank you for your promise to us in the resurrection of your Son. By retracing the steps of his passion and death, and following his path through suffering to glory, may we be inspired to lead lives on earth which are pleasing to you, and one day be found worthy to praise you for ever in our heavenly home.*

Leader: For ourselves, and for all those on pilgrimage here in Lourdes, that through Mary's intercession and the prayers of Saint Bernadette, we may be made worthy of the promises of Christ:

Lord, in your mercy *(sung)*

All: **Hear our prayer** *(sung)*

All: **I love you, Jesus my love, above all things; I repent with my whole heart for having offended you. Never permit me to separate myself from you again. Grant that I may love you always and then do with me what you will.**

EVENING PRAYER : COMMUNAL

INTRODUCTION

Leader: O God, come to our aid.

All: **O Lord, make haste to help us.**
Glory be to the Father and to the Son and to the Holy Spirit, as it was in the beginning, is now and ever shall be, world without end. Amen. (Alleluia)

HYMN

The following hymn may be used, or another suitable hymn or song chosen from the selection on pages 218-298

> Before the light of evening fades
> We pray, O Lord of all,
> That by your love we may be saved
> From every grievous fall.
>
> Repel the terrors of the night
> And Satan's power of guile,
> Impose a calm and restful sleep
> That nothing may defile.
>
> Most Holy Father, grant our prayer
> Through Christ your only Son,
> That in your Spirit we may live
> And praise you ever One.

Other psalms, canticles, scripture readings and prayers may be chosen. If the antiphons are used, they are sung (or said) before and after each psalm or canticle.

PSALMODY

Psalm 109

Antiphon 1

The Lord will send his mighty sceptre from Sion, and he will rule for ever. (Alleluia)

The Lord's revelation to my Master:
"Sit on my right:
your foes I will put beneath your feet."

The Lord will wield from Sion
your sceptre of power:
rule in the midst of all your foes.

A prince from the day of your birth
on the holy mountains;
from the womb before the dawn I begot you.

The Lord has sworn an oath he will not change.
"You are a priest for ever,
a priest like Melchisedek of old."

The Master standing at your right hand
will shatter kings in the day of his great wrath.

He shall drink from the stream by the wayside
and therefore he shall lift up his head.

Glory be to the Father and to the Son
and to the Holy Spirit.
As it was in the beginning, is now and ever shall be,
world without end. Amen.

Antiphon I

The Lord will send his mighty sceptre from Sion, and he will rule for ever. (Alleluia)

Psalm 113

Antiphon II

The earth trembled before the Lord. (Alleluia)

When Israel came forth from Egypt,
Jacob's sons from an alien people,
Judah became the Lord's temple,
Israel became his kingdom.
The sea fled at the sight:
the Jordan turned back on its course.

the mountains leapt like rams
and the hills like yearling sheep.

Why was it, sea, that you fled,
that you turned back, Jordan, on your course?
Mountains, that you leapt like rams,
hills, like yearling sheep?

Tremble, O earth, before the Lord,
in the presence of the God of Jacob,
who turns the rock into a pool
and flint into a spring of water.

Glory be to the Father and to the Son
and to the Holy Spirit.
As it was in the beginning, is now and ever shall be,
world without end. Amen.

Antiphon II

The earth trembled before the Lord. (Alleluia)

Canticle of Revelation (19:1,2,5-7) *(Except during Lent)*

Antiphon III

The Lord is King, our God, the Almighty! Alleluia.

Alleluia.
Salvation and glory and power belong to our God,
Alleluia. His judgements are true and just.
Alleluia, alleluia.

Alleluia.
Praise our God, all you his servants, Alleluia.
You who fear him, small and great.
Alleluia, alleluia.

Alleluia.
The Lord our God, the Almighty, reigns, Alleluia.
Let us rejoice and exult and give him the glory.
Alleluia, alleluia.

Alleluia.
The marriage of the Lamb has come, Alleluia.
And his bride has made herself ready.
Alleluia, alleluia.

Glory be to the Father and to the Son
and to the Holy Spirit.
As it was in the beginning, is now and ever shall be,
world without end. Amen.

Antiphon III

The Lord is King, our God, the Almighty! Alleluia.

Canticle of Peter (I Peter 2:21-24)   (*During Lent*)

Antiphon III

He carried our sins in his own body on the cross, so that
we might die to sin and live for holiness.

Christ suffered for you,
leaving you an example
that you should follow in his steps.

He committed no sin;
no guile was found on his lips.
When he was reviled,
he did not revile in return.

When he suffered,
he did not threaten;
but he trusted to him
who judges justly.

He himself bore our sins
in his body on the tree,
that we might die to sin
and live to righteousness.

By his wounds you have been healed.

Glory be to the Father and to the Son
and to the Holy Spirit.
As it was in the beginning, is now and ever shall be,
world without end. Amen.

Antiphon III

He carried our sins in his own body on the cross, so that we might die to sin and live for holiness.

SCRIPTURE READING   (II Corinthians 1:3-4)

Let us give thanks to the God and Father of our Lord Jesus Christ, the merciful Father, the God from whom all help comes! He helps us in all our troubles, so that we are able to help those who have all kinds of troubles, using the same help that we ourselves have received from God.

SHORT RESPONSORY

Leader: Blessed are you, O Lord, in the vault of heaven.
All: **Blessed are you, O Lord, in the vault of heaven.**
Leader: You are exalted and glorified above all else for ever.
All: **In the vault of heaven**
Leader: Glory be to the Father and to the Son and to the Holy Spirit.
All: **Blessed are you, O Lord, in the vault of heaven.**

CANTICLE OF MARY (Magnificat) (*Luke* 1:46-55)

Antiphon

You have only one master and he is in heaven: Christ the Lord.

My soul glorifies the Lord,
my spirit rejoices in God, my Saviour.
He looks on his servant in her lowliness;
henceforth all ages will call me blessed.

The Almighty works marvels for me.
Holy his name!
His mercy is from age to age,
on those who fear him.

He puts forth his arm in strength
and scatters the proud-hearted.
He casts the mighty from their thrones
and raises the lowly.

He fills the starving with good things,
sends the rich away empty.

He protects Israel, his servant,
remembering his mercy,
the mercy promised to our fathers,
to Abraham and his sons for ever.

Praise the Father, the Son and Holy Spirit,
both now and for ever, world without end.

Antiphon

You have only one master and he is in heaven: Christ the Lord.

INTERCESSIONS

Leader: Let us bring our evening prayer before Christ, who is the one mediator between us and our merciful God.

All: **O Lord, let our prayer rise before you like incense.**

Leader: That the Church may be a sign to all nations of the goodness of God:

All: **O Lord, let our prayer rise before you like incense.**

Leader: For those whom we have met during this day, that they may see Christ in us:

All: **O Lord, let our prayer rise before you like incense.**

Leader: For peace in our world, and freedom from anxiety for those suffering from oppression:

All: **O Lord, let our prayer rise before you like incense.**

Leader: For the Pope, for our bishops, priests and deacons, and for those who exercise ministry within the Church:

All: **O Lord, let our prayer rise before you like incense.**

Leader: For those who will die during this night, that they may enjoy the glory of the resurrection:

All: **O Lord, let our prayer rise before you like incense.**

Pause for any other intentions…

All: **Our Father...**

Leader: Lord of the evening,
             grant us the grace
             to keep our minds fixed on you,
             that, amid the changes of this passing world,
             we may place our trust firmly in your word,
             and come to the joys which you have promised,
             in the kingdom where you live and reign,
             with Christ and the Holy Spirit,
             one God for ever and ever.

All: **Amen.**

CONCLUSION

Leader: May almighty God bless us,
             the Father, and the Son,
             and the Holy Spirit.

All: **Amen.**

Leader: Let us bless the Lord.

All: **Thanks be to God.**

NIGHT PRAYER : INDIVIDUAL

This form of Night Prayer, based loosely on Compline from the Divine Office of the Church, offers a simple pattern which can be used or adapted by an individual at any time of the year. It would normally be recited last thing at night, just before retiring to sleep. For the earlier Evening Prayer (Vespers), celebrated communally and taken from the Divine Office, see pages 177-183.

SIGN OF THE CROSS

> In the name of the Father who created me,
> the Son who set me free,
> and the Holy Spirit who sustains me.
> Amen.

EXAMINATION OF CONSCIENCE

A few moments of reflection to look over the day past and to ask God's pardon for any sins committed. Then:

> Lord, who hast formed me out of mud,
> And hast redeemed me through thy blood,
> And sanctified me to do good:
> *Forgive my sins, O Father God.*

> Purge all my sins done heretofore,
> For I confess my heavy score,
> And I will strive to sin no more:
> *Have mercy on me, Son of God.*

> Enrich my heart, mouth, hands in me,
> With faith, with hope, with charity,
> That I may run, rise, rest with thee:
> *Breathe life into me, Spirit Lord.*

THANKSGIVING

Psalm 4

> When I call, answer me, O God of justice;
> from anguish you released me, have mercy and hear me!

O men, how long will your hearts be closed,
will you love what is futile and seek what is false?

It is the Lord who grants favours to those whom he loves;
the Lord hears me whenever I call him.

Fear him; do not sin; ponder on your bed and be still.
Make justice your sacrifice and trust in the Lord.

"What can bring us happiness?" many say.
Let the light of your face shine on us, O Lord.

You have put into my heart a greater joy
than they have from abundance of corn and new wine.

I will lie down in peace and sleep comes at once
for you alone, Lord, make me dwell in safety.

Glory be to the Father, and to the Son, and to the Holy
Spirit.
As it was in the beginning, is now and ever shall be,
world without end. Amen.

GOD'S WORD   (*Deuteronomy 6·4-7*)

Hear, O Israel: The Lord is our God, the Lord alone. You shall
love the Lord your God with all your heart, and with all your
soul, and with all your might. Keep these words that I am
commanding you today in your heart. Recite them to your
children and talk about them when you are at home and
when you are away, when you lie down and when you rise.

SHORT RESPONSORY

Into your hands, Lord, I commend my spirit.
You have redeemed me, Lord God of truth.

Into your hands, Lord, I commend my spirit.

Glory be to the Father,
and to the Son, and to the Holy Spirit.

Into your hands, Lord, I commend my spirit.

NUNC DIMITTIS (*Luke 2:29-32*)

The Nunc Dimittis is the prayer said by the old man, Simeon, who came to see the infant Jesus being presented in the Temple:

> At last, all-powerful Master,
> you give leave to your servant
> to go in peace, according to your promise.

> For my eyes have seen your salvation
> which you have prepared for all nations,
> the light to enlighten the Gentiles
> and give glory to Israel, your people.

> Glory be to the Father, and to the Son, and to the Holy Spirit.
> As it was in the beginning, is now and ever shall be,
> world without end. Amen.

CONCLUDING BLESSING-PRAYER

> Lord of the night,
> protect me while I am awake
> and guard me while I sleep.
> May your blessing be upon me,
> that I may keep watch with Christ
> and rest with him in peace,
> for he is Lord, now and forever.
> Amen.

PART FIVE

"PRAY FOR SINNERS"

Blessing for Departing Pilgrims

Blessing for Returning Pilgrims

Prayers for Various Occasions

Songs, Hymns and Refrains

BLESSING FOR DEPARTING PILGRIMS

The following Blessing Service is designed for use either on the day of departure or at a gathering of pilgrims sometime prior to the pilgrimage. It has been written in such a way that it may be led by anyone: bishop, priest, deacon or layperson.

If there is to be no public celebration, then it can easily be adapted for use by the individual pilgrim. Using whatever elements seem suitable, the individual can read and reflect on the word of God, ask for conversion, spiritual growth and a sense of mission, pray for the intentions of the pilgrimage, and invoke God's blessing for safe-keeping on the journey.

INTRODUCTION

A suitable song may be sung from the selection given on pp.218-298.

Leader: Blessed be the Lord who keeps us safe.

All: **Blessed be God forever**

In a few words the leader welcomes everyone and reminds them of what they are about to undertake: a journey towards God with a purpose; a visit to a holy place; a recommitment to penance, poverty, prayer and participation in the life of the Church

WORD OF GOD

Listen to the word of God from the second letter of St Paul to the Corinthians (II *Cor* 5:6-10)

So we are always confident; even though we know that while we are at home in the body we are away from the Lord - for we walk by faith, not by sight. Yes, we do have confidence, and we would rather be away from the body and at home with the Lord. So whether we are at home or away, we make it our aim to please him. For all of us must appear before the judgement seat of Christ, so that each may receive recompense for what has been done in the body, good or evil.
The word of the Lord.

All: **Thanks be to God.**

All respond to this reading by a song or psalm such as the following:

Psalm 120

R.   **The Lord will guard our going and coming both now and forever.**

1.   I lift up my eyes to the mountains:
       from where shall come my help?
       My help shall come from the Lord
       who made heaven and earth.

2.   May he never allow you to stumble!
       Let him sleep not, your guard.
       No, he sleeps not nor slumbers,
       Israel's guard.

3.   The Lord is your guard and your shade;
       at your right side he stands.
       By day the sun shall not smite you
       nor the moon in the night.

4.   The Lord will guard you from evil,
       he will guard your soul.
       The Lord will guard your going and coming
       both now and forever.

The leader, or some other suitable person, may give a brief reflection on the scripture which has just been proclaimed.

INTERCESSIONS

Leader: We have heard the word of God. Now let us
          come before the Lord bringing our needs and
          our prayers.
          We pray that God will watch over our pilgrimage
          to Lourdes, and that we may arrive safely at our
          destination.
          Lord, in your mercy:

All: **Hear our prayer.**

Leader: We pray for a true spirit of penance, that this
          pilgrimage may lead us to deeper conversion.

Lord, in your mercy:

All: **Hear our prayer.**

Leader: We pray for the sick on our pilgrimage, and for the handmaids and brancardiers who will look after their needs.
Lord, in your mercy:

All: **Hear our prayer.**

Leader: We pray for those who have organized and arranged our pilgrimage, and those who will lead us in worship and spiritual exercises.
Lord, in your mercy:

All: **Hear our prayer.**

Leader: We pray for those who will remain at home, those who have made it possible for us to undertake the pilgrimage, and those who will be supporting us with their prayers.
Lord, in your mercy:

All: **Hear our prayer.**

Leader: Our Lady of Lourdes:
All: **Hear our prayer.**

Leader: St Bernadette:
All: **Hear our prayer.**

BLESSING

Leader: God of our journey,
be with us on this pilgrimage,
and guide our feet along your path of life.
Be our companion by day and by night;
may we feel your presence at our side.
Keep us safe, and give us your blessing,
that our journey, begun in faith,
may reach its true completion
through Christ our Lord.

All: **Amen.**

A suitable song may conclude the Blessing Service.

BLESSING FOR RETURNING PILGRIMS

This service follows the same principles as the Blessing for Departing Pilgrims on pages 191-193, and may be celebrated publicly or adapted for individual use by pilgrims. It is anticipated that this simple service be celebrated informally on the last day of the pilgrimage, and that it not detract from the importance of the final pilgrimage Mass.

INTRODUCTION

A suitable song may be sung from the selection given on pp 218-298.

Leader: Blessed be the Lord who will lead us home rejoicing.

All: **Blessed be God forever.**

In a few words the leader welcomes everyone and reminds them of what they have undertaken, of the salient happenings of their time together, of the blessings that have been apparent on the pilgrimage, and of the hidden way in which God continues to move among those who truly seek the grace of a pilgrimage.

WORD OF GOD

Listen to the word of God from the holy Gospel according to Luke (*Luke* 24:32-36)

The disciples (who had met Jesus on the road to Emmaus) said to each other, "Were not our hearts burning within us while he was talking to us on the road, while he was opening the scriptures to us?" That same hour they got up and returned to Jerusalem; and they found the eleven and their companions gathered together. They were saying, "The Lord has risen indeed, and he has appeared to Simon!" Then they told what had happened on the road, and how he had been made known to them in the breaking of the bread.

The Gospel of the Lord.

All: **Praise to you, Lord Jesus Christ.**

All respond to this reading by a song or psalm such as the following:

Psalm 150

R.   **Let everything that lives**
     give praise to the Lord.

1   Praise God in his holy place,
     praise him in his mighty heavens.
     Praise him for his powerful deeds,
     praise his surpassing greatness. R.

2   O praise him with sound of trumpet,
     praise him with lute and harp.
     Praise him with timbrel and dance,
     praise him with strings and pipes. R.

3   O praise him with resounding cymbals,
     praise him with clashing of cymbals.
     Let everything that lives and that breathes
     praise the name of the Lord. R.

The leader, or some other suitable person, may give a brief reflection on the scripture that has just been proclaimed.

INTERCESSIONS

Leader: We have heard the word of God. Now let us
          come before the Lord bringing our needs and
          our prayers.

          Let us pray that we may have a safe return
          journey to our homes and loved ones.
          We turn to you, O Lord:

All: **Hear and answer our prayer**

Leader: Let us pray for those whose dedicated service
          has made our pilgrimage a time of grace and
          favour.
          We turn to you, O Lord:

All: **Hear and answer our prayer**

Leader: Let us pray for peoples of all nationalities whom we have met during our stay here in Lourdes, for peace and prosperity in their lands.
We turn to you, O Lord:

All: **Hear and answer our prayer**

Leader: Let us pray for those who await us back home, and for ourselves that we may reflect to them the vision of God we have experienced on this pilgrimage.
We turn to you, O Lord:

All: **Hear and answer our prayer**

Leader: Our Lady of Lourdes:
All: **Pray for us.**

Leader: St Bernadette:
All: **Pray for us.**

BLESSING

Leader: God of our journey,
we thank you for the graces
and the favours of our pilgrimage.
As we return home, bless us on our way.
May we continue to walk faithfully
along the pathways of life,
until we reach the everlasting city
in the kingdom which is to come,
where you are Lord,
for ever and ever.

All: **Amen.**

A suitable song may conclude the Blessing Service.

PRAYERS FOR VARIOUS OCCASIONS

GENERAL

Morning Offering
O Jesus, through the most pure heart of Mary, I offer you all the prayers, thoughts, works and sufferings of this day.

Act of Contrition
O my God, because you are so good, I am very sorry that I have sinned against you, and by the help of your grace I will try not to sin again.

Act of Faith
My God, I believe in you and all that your Church teaches, because you have said it, and your word is true.

Act of Hope
My God, I hope in you, for grace and for glory, because of your promises, your mercy and power.

Act of Charity
O my God, I love you with my whole heart and above all things, because you are infinitely good and perect; and I love my neighbour as myself for love of you. Grant that I may love you more and more in this life, and in the next for eternity.

The Grace
The grace of our Lord Jesus Christ, and the love of God, and the fellowship of the Holy Spirit, be with us all evermore. Amen.

Grace before Meals
Bless us, O Lord, and these your gifts which we are about to receive from your goodness, through Christ our Lord. Amen.

Grace after Meals

We give you thanks, almighty God, for these and all your benefits which we have received through Christ our Lord. Amen.

Prayer to the Holy Spirit

Come, Holy Spirit, fill the hearts of your faithful.
And kindle in them the fire of your love.
Send forth your Spirit and they shall be created.
And you will renew the face of the earth.

Let us pray:
Lord, by the light of the Holy Spirit
you have taught the hearts of your faithful.
In the same Spirit
help us to relish what is right
and always rejoice in your consolation.
Through Christ our Lord. Amen.

Apostles' Creed

I believe in God, the Father almighty,
creator of heaven and earth.

I believe in Jesus Christ, his only Son, our Lord.
He was conceived by the power of the Holy Spirit
and born of the Virgin Mary.
He suffered under Pontius Pilate,
was crucified, died, and was buried.
He descended to the dead.
On the third day he rose again.
He ascended into heaven,
and is seated at the right hand of the Father.
He will come again to judge the living and the dead.

I believe in the Holy Spirit,
the holy catholic Church,
the communion of saints,
the forgiveness of sins,
the resurrection of the body,
and the life everlasting. Amen.

TO THE VIRGIN MARY

The Rosary

The Five Joyful Mysteries

1   **The Annunciation** (*Luke* 1:26-38)
    The Angel Gabriel announced to Mary that she would be the Virgin Mother of the one who would save God's people.

2   **The Visitation** (*Luke* 1:39-56)
    Mary goes to see her cousin Elizabeth, who herself is expecting a child - John the Baptist.

3   **The Nativity** (*Luke* 2:1-20)
    Jesus is born in Bethlehem and God comes to dwell in our midst as Emmanuel.

4   **The Presentation in the Temple** (*Luke* 2:22-32)
    Mary and Joseph fulfil the law and Jesus is presented in the Temple. Simeon and Anna praise God when they see the child.

5   **The Finding of the Jesus in the Temple** (*Luke* 2.41-52)
    Mary and Joseph are relieved and the boy Jesus hints at his future mission.

The Five Sorrowful Mysteries

1   **The Agony in the Garden** (Luke 22:39-46)
    Jesus accepts the suffering knowing that God can bring good from his passion and death.

2   **The Scourging at the Pillar** (Matthew 27:24-26)
    Although Pilate knew Jesus was innocent of any crime, he had him flogged to save his own position.

3   **The Crowning with Thorns** (Matthew 27:27-31)
    Jesus is dressed mockingly in the robes of a king, with reeds for a sceptre and thorns for a crown.

4   **The Carrying of the Cross** (Matthew 27:32-38)
    What was a symbol of execution to the onlookers became the instrument by which Jesus would save the life of the world.

5   **The Crucifixion** (Matthew 27:45-50)
Jesus dies, abandoned by almost all, and puts his trust in the will of his Father.

The Five Glorious Mysteries

1   **The Resurrection** (John 20:1-10)
The tomb is empty, the grave-clothes could not bind him, for he is risen as he said.

2   **The Ascension** (Mark 16:19-20)
After giving the command to go and teach all nations, Jesus ascends to his Father in heaven to complete his mission by sending the Spirit.

3   **The Descent of the Holy Spirit** (Acts 2:1-4)
The power of the Holy Spirit is given to the Church to transform the disciples from timidity to boldness.

4   **The Assumption** (Ephesians 1:1-6)
Mary, the first to believe in the message of the Incarnation, now shares the promised joy and the glory of her Son's reign in heaven.

5   **The Crowning of Mary in Heaven** (Revelation 12:1-6)
Mary represents the Church which is now set free by Christ and the whole of redeemed creation which awaits the crowning glory of the Last Day.

The Five Luminous Mysteries

1   **The Baptism in the Jordan** (Matthew 3: 13-17)
Jesus prepares himself to undertake the mission entrusted to him by his Father and is strengthened by the Holy Spirit for what is to come.

2   **The Wedding of Cana** (John 2: 1-12)
Jesus performs his first miracle as he turns water into wine, allowing his glory to be seen and showing himself to be sent by God

3   **The Proclamation of the Kingdom of God** (Mark 1: 14-15)
Jesus begins to preach that the Kingdom of God is close at hand and invites his hearers to repent and believe in the Gospel.

4   **The Transfiguration** (*Mark* 9: 2-8)
Jesus is transfigured on the mountain and his glory is revealed to the apostles as he talks with Moses and Elijah.

5   **The Institution of the Eucharist** (*Luke* 22: 14-20)
As a lasting memorial of his presence Jesus institutes the Eucharist and commands us to celebrate it in memory of him by eating and drinking his body and blood.

The Angelus

The Angel of the Lord declared unto Mary:
And she conceived of the Holy Spirit.
Hail Mary…

Behold the handmaid of the Lord:
Be it done unto me according to your word.
Hail Mary…

And the Word was made flesh:
And dwelt among us.
Hail Mary…

Pray for us, O holy Mother of God
That we may be made worthy of the promises of Christ.

Let us pray:
Pour forth, we beseech you, O Lord, your grace into our hearts, that we, to whom the Incarnation of Christ your Son was made known by the message of angel, may by his passion and cross be brought to the glory of his resurrection, through the same Christ our Lord. Amen.

Memorare

Remember, O most loving Virgin Mary, that it is a thing unheard of, that anyone ever had recourse to your protection, implored your help or sought your intercession, and was left forsaken. Filled, therefore, with confidence in your goodness, I fly to you, O Mother, Virgin of Virgins. To you I come; before you I stand, a sorrowful sinner. Despise not my poor words, O Mother of the Word of God, but graciously hear and grant my prayer. Amen.

Hail Holy Queen

Hail, Holy Queen, mother of mercy; hail, our life, our sweetness and our hope. To you do we cry, poor banished children of Eve. To you do we send up our sighs, mourning and weeping in this vale of tears. Turn then, most gracious advocate, your eyes of mercy towards us; and after this our exile, show unto us the blessed fruit of your womb, Jesus. O clement, O loving, O sweet Virgin Mary.

Pray for us, O holy Mother of God.
That we may be made worthy of the promises of Christ.

(When this prayer is said at the end of the Rosary, the following is added:)

Let us pray:

O God, whose only-begotten Son, by his life, death, and resurrection has purchased for us the rewards of eternal life; grant, we beseech you, that, meditating upon these mysteries of the most holy Rosary of the Blessed Virgin Mary, we may both imitate what they contain and obtain what they promise. Through the same Christ our Lord. Amen.

Regina Coeli *(Replaces Hail Holy Queen during Eastertime)*

O Queen of heaven, rejoice! Alleluia.
For he whom you did merit to bear, Alleluia,
Has risen as he said. Alleuia.
Pray for us to God. Alleuia.
Rejoice and be glad, O Virgin Mary, Alleuia,
For the Lord has risen indeed. Alleluia.

Let us pray:
O God, who gave joy to the world through the resurrection of your Son our Lord Jesus Christ, grant that we may obtain, through his Virgin Mother, Mary, the joys of everlasting life. Through the same Christ our Lord. Amen.

FOR THE DEAD

Eternal rest grant unto them, O Lord,
And let perpetual light shine upon them.
May they rest in peace. Amen.

Out of the depths I cry to you, O Lord,
Lord, hear my voice!
O let your ears be attentive
to the voice of my pleading.

If you, O Lord, should mark our guilt,
Lord, who would survive?
But with you is found forgiveness:
for this we revere you.

My soul is waiting for the Lord,
I count on his word.
My soul is longing for the Lord
more than watchman for daybreak.
Let the watchman count on daybreak
and Israel on the Lord.

Because with the Lord there is mercy,
and fullness of redemption,
Israel indeed he will redeem
from all its iniquity.

Glory be to the Father,
and to the Son, and to the Holy Spirit:
as it was in the beginning, is now, and ever shall be,
world without end. Amen. (*De Profundis, Psalm* 129)

May the choirs of angels
come to greet you;
may they speed you to Paradise.
May the Lord enfold you
in his mercy;
may you find eternal life.

PRAYERS FROM SCRIPTURE

Faith

Lord, I believe!
Help my unbelief. (*Mark* 9:25)

In God alone is my soul at rest;
my help comes from him.
He alone is my rock, my stronghold
my fortress; I stand firm. (*Psalm* 61:2-3)

Sorrow

God of mercy and compassion,
slow to anger, O Lord,
abounding in love and truth,
turn and take pity on me. (*Psalm* 85:15-16)

Have mercy on me, God,
in your kindness.
In your compassion
blot out my offence. (*Psalm* 50:3)

Joy

Like the deer that yearns
for running streams,
so my soul is yearning
for you, my God. (*Psalm* 41:2)

My heart rejoices, and my soul is glad;
even my body shall rest in safety.
You will show me the path of life,
the fullness of joy in your presence,
at your right hand happiness for ever. (*Psalm* 15:9-11)

Forgiveness

Be compassionate as your Father is compassionate. (*Luke* 6:36)

Lord, do not reprove me in your anger,
or punish me in your rage.
Have mercy on me, Lord, for my strength fails;
heal and forgive me. (*Psalm* 6:2-3)

Anxiety

My God, my God,
do not leave me alone in my distress;
come close, there is no one else to help. (Psalm 21:12)

Can a woman forget the child nursing at her breast,
or show no compassion for the child of her womb?
Well, even if these do forget,
I will never forget you, says the Lord. (Isaiah 49:15)

Peace

Lord mine is not a proud heart,
and my eyes are not boastful.
I have set my soul in peace and calm,
like a weaned child on its mother's breast. (Psalm 130:1-2)

Blessed are the peacmakers,
for they shall be called the children of God. (Matthew 5:9)

Love

Our love is not to be just words and mere talk,
but something real and active. (1 John 3:18)

A new commandment I give to you;
love one another;
as I have loved you,
so you also must love one another.
By this love you have for one another,
all will know that you are my disciples. (John 13:34-35)

FOR THE NEEDS OF THE CHURCH

The Pope

O God, the shepherd and ruler of all the faithful,
look down favourably on your servant Pope N,
whom you have been pleased to appoint pastor of your
Church;
grant, we beseech you,
that he may benefit both by word and example

those over whom he is set,
and thus attain life eternal,
together with the flock committed to his care.

Bishops

Lord,
we pray to you for N, our bishop.
May he lead our diocese by his word and example,
and may he be a wise pastor for all those in his care.
Bless him, keep him safe, and strengthen him in faith.

Priests and deacons

Father,
we thank you for the priests and deacons
who serve the people of our diocese.
Make them effective witnesses to your word,
and give them joy in their service,
that in the power of your Holy Spirit
they may bring lasting good to your Church.

Married people

Lord,
bless all married couples.
May they know that you call them
to be signs of your unconditional love for your world.
In good times may they thank you and praise you.
When times become hard, may they know you are near.
May they reach old age
surrounded by their children's children,
and one day be united for ever
in the marriage feast of heaven.

Religious vocations

Jesus, you came to search out and save what was lost,
and to offer fullness of life to those who seek you.
Inspire the hearts of men and women today
to serve you as priests, deacons and religious.

Help them to discern your call,
and having called them,
make them strong in their resolve to follow you.

Christian Unity

Lord Jesus Christ, you said to your apostles, "I leave you peace, peace is my gift to you." Grant that we may all be one, as you and the Father are one. Do not look upon our sins but upon the faith of your Church, and grant us all that peace and unity which is according to your will.

PRAYERS OF THE SAINTS

I sing as I arise today!
I call upon my Creator's might
The will of God to be my guide,
The eye of God to be my sight,
The word of God to be my speech,
The hand of God to be my stay,
The shield of God to be my strength
The path of God to be my way. (St *Patrick*)

Holy Spirit,
make me ready to listen
and willing to do what you ask of me,
that I may learn to obey
the commands of the Father,
because of Jesus Christ our Saviour. (St *Bede*)

Lord, you have made us for yourself,
and our hearts are restless
until they find their home in you. (St *Augustine*)

Late have I loved you,
O Beauty ever ancient, ever new,
Late have I loved you.
You were within me,
But I was outside;
And it was there that I searched for you.

In my unloveliness I plunged
Into the lovely things which you created.
You were with me,
But I was not with you. (St *Augustine*)

Let nothing disturb you,
nothing alarm you;
all things are passing;
God never changes;
Patient endurance
attains to all things;
Whoever possesses God
wants for nothing;
God alone suffices. (St *Teresa of Avila*)

Jesu, blessed Jesu, strengthen me in soul and body, that I
may not fail you. (St *John Paine*)

O blessed Jesu, make me understand and remember that
whatsoever we gain, if we lose you, all is lost, and
whatsoever we lose, if we gain you, all is gained.
(St *Thomas Cottam*)

Lord, make me an instrument of your peace:
Where there is hatred, let me sow love;
where there is injury, let me sow pardon;
where there is doubt, let me sow faith;
where there is despair, let me give hope;
where there is darkness, let me bring light;
where there is sadness, let me give joy.
O Divine Master, grant that I may try
not to be comforted, but to comfort;
not to be understood, but to understand;
not to be loved, but to love.
Because it is in giving that we receive;
it is in forgiving that we are forgiven,
and it is in dying that we rise to eternal life.
(*Based on St Francis of Assisi*)

Take from me, good Lord, this lukewarm fashion,
or rather key-cold manner of meditation
and this dullness in praying to you.
And give me warmth, delight and life in thinking about you.
(St Thomas More)

Lord, you are calling me to come to you,
and I am coming to you -
not with any merits of my own,
but only with your mercy.
I am begging you for this mercy
in virtue of your Son's most sweet blood.

(St Catherine of Siena)

Lord, give me patience in tribulation.
Let the memory of your Passion,
and of those bitter pains you suffered for me,
strengthen my patience and support me in this tribulation
and adversity. (St John Forest)

Jesus, grant me the grace to love you.
O blessed Jesu, make me love you entirely.
O blessed Jesu, let me deeply consider your love for me.
O blessed Jesu, give me the grace to thank you for your gifts.
Sweet Jesu, possess my heart,
hold it and keep it for yourself alone. (St John Fisher)

Teach us, good Lord, to serve you as you deserve;
to give and not to count the cost;
to fight and not to heed the wounds;
to toil and not to seek for rest;
to labour and to ask for no reward,
save that of knowing that we do your will;
through Christ our Lord. (St Ignatius)

Take, Lord, all my liberty.
Receive my memory, my understanding
and my whole will.
Whatever I have and possess,
you have given me;

to you I restore it wholly,
and to your will I utterly surrender
for my direction.
Give me the love of you only,
with your grace,
and I am rich enough;
nor do I ask anything besides. (St *Ignatius*)

Thanks be to you, my Lord Jesus Christ,
for all the benefits
which you have given me,
for all the pains and insults
which you have borne for me.
O most merciful Redeemer, Friend and Brother,
may I know you more clearly,
love you more dearly,
follow you more nearly,
day by day. (St *Richard of Chichester*)

PRAYERS FOR MOMENTS IN LOURDES

Dedication of handmaids, brancardiers and helpers

Lord Jesus,
I give you my hands to do your work,
and my feet to go your way.
I give you my eyes to see as you do,
and my tongue to speak your words.
I give you my mind that you may think in me,
and my spirit that you may pray in me.
Above all, I give you my heart
that in me you may love your Father and all humankind.
I give you my whole self that you may grow in me,
so that it is you, Lord Jesus,
who live and work and pray in me.

(*Based on the Grail Prayer*)

Make us worthy, Lord,
to serve our fellow men throughout the world
who live and die in poverty and hunger.
Give them through our hands this day their daily bread,
and, by our understanding love,
give peace and joy.   (*Mother Teresa of Calcutta*)

O God, teach us to live together
in love and joy and peace,
to check all bitterness,
to disown discouragement,
to practise thanksgiving,
and to leap with joy to any task for others.
Strengthen the good thing thus begun,
that with gallant and high-hearted happiness
we may look for your kingdom in the wills of men.
Through Jesus Christ our Lord. (*Toc H*)

At the Grotto

Dedication for service

O Lord, you are my God,
and for you I long with all my heart.
As I stand before you in this place
where the Virgin Mary appeared to Bernadette,
I renew my desire to follow wherever you may lead.
Take me and use me for your Gospel.
Grant me the grace to overcome my weaknesses;
to bear my burdens lightly;
to be attentive to your voice;
and to be zealous in your service.
During my stay in Lourdes, give me
that faith which will never remain silent,
that hope which will never cease to trust,
that love which will burn always brightly,
and that joy which delights in your Church.

For those who asked for prayers

So many people have asked me to pray for them, Lord, and now I am here I cannot remember all their names and their intentions. But you know the names of all those whom you have made, and they are close to you, held in the palm of your hands.

In silence I place them before you now...

In this holy place, I pray also for:
the sick at home and in hospital,
and those who are with us on this pilgrimage;
children who have never known full health,
and parents who look after them;

our diocese and parish back home, the priests and people,
our schools, catechists, ministers and those in our church
organizations;

those who are seeking work, those finding it hard to make
ends meet, and those who have no roof over their head;
those undergoing marriage difficulties,
those who have been abused in any way,
and those who are looking for love;

people who are approaching death with fear,
those with terminal illnesses,
and those who have recently lost a loved one;

countries where people have insufficient food and water,
those who lack medical attention
and those who suffer unjust regimes;

all those who make life worth living, my own family
members, my friends and neighbours, those at work, and
those who are there when I need them most;

the whole Church of God scattered throughout the world,
that it may be a sign to the world that your Son is risen
and offers us life to the full;

All these needs, Lord, and those I cannot now remember, I
bring before you in the name of Christ our Lord. Amen.

In pain

Jesus, you underwent the agony of the Cross and you know the sickness and pain that I have had recently. Sometimes I do not understand why it has to be, but I know that you will never allow me to suffer for no reason at all. Here at the Grotto I offer you my body and mind that you may use them as you see fit and for the good of others. But when the pain seems overbearing, Lord, do not let me give in to self-pity. Lighten the burden when this happens and remind me of the presence I can feel here and now.

Mental illness

Lord, I know that my mind is not what it was. I feel troubled and I lack the sparkle which I once took for granted. I am grateful for those who look after me, even though I sometimes become irritated when I feel they are swamping me. In this holy place I ask you to restore me to my former self, but if this is not to be, then help me to get the most out of each new day which you bring. You know that sometimes I find it hard to make the effort, but at this moment I am telling you that I want always to love you, and I thank you for being my God.

Terminal illness

It cannot be long now, Lord, but only you know the length of my days. I do not relish dying, because there are so many things I want to be part of, and so many people I do not want to leave. But I remember the promise that those who believe in your Son Jesus, even though they die, will live. I thank you for all the good things that my life has been blessed with; for family and friends, for those who today are seeing to my daily needs; for the medical staff here and at home who give me such great encouragement. Keep me strong in faith and love. Let me not experience great pain, and be there to call me to the everlasting happiness of heaven, in the company of those who have gone before me, with Our Lady of Lourdes and all the saints.

At the baths

O Lord, you know how nervous I have become
and how anxious
about being moved or carried by others.
Take away my fear,
and let me remember
that I am in the hands of those
who have great experience
and who do their task with loving care.
Let my bathing in the water
be a sign of my faith in you.
Ease my pain, Lord;
help me to trust,
and give me the joy of feeling you near.

O God, to whom all hearts are open,
all desires known,
and from whom no secrets are hidden,
cleanse the thoughts of our hearts
by the outpouring of your Holy Spirit,
that every thought and word of ours
may begin from you,
and in you be perfectly completed,
through Christ our Lord. Amen.

Waiting for events to begin

O gracious and holy Father,
give us the wisdom to perceive you,
intelligence to understand you,
diligence to seek you,
patience to wait for you,
eyes to behold you,
a heart to meditate upon you,
and a life to proclaim you;
through the power of the Spirit
of Jesus Christ our Lord. (*St Benedict*)

God be in my head, and in my understanding;
God be in mine eyes, and in my looking;
God be in my mouth, and in my speaking;
God be in my heart, and in my thinking;
God be at mine end, and at my departing. (*Book of Hours*)

When feeling distracted

I hand over to your care, Lord,
my soul and body,
my mind and thoughts,
my prayers and my hopes,
my health and my work,
my life and my death,
my parents and my family,
my friends and my neighbours,
my country and all men.
Today and always. (*Lancelot Andrews*)

When the heart is hard and parched up,
come upon me with a shower of mercy.
When grace is lost from life,
come with a burst of song.
When tumultuous work raises its din on all sides,
shutting me out from beyond,
come to me, my Lord of silence,
with thy peace and rest.
When my beggarly heart sits crouched,
shut up in a corner,
break open the door, my king,
and come with the ceremony of a king.
When desire blinds the mind with delusion and dust,
O thou holy one, thou wakeful,
come with thy light and thy thunder. (*Tagore*)

When feeling ill

O God, our Father, bless and help me
in the illness which has come upon me.
Give me courage and patience,
endurance and cheerfulness
to bear all weakness and pain;
and give me the mind at rest,
which will make my recovery all the quicker.

Give to all doctors, surgeons and nurses who attend me
skill on their hands, wisdom in their minds,
and gentleness and sympathy in their hearts.

Help me not to worry too much,
but to leave myself in the hands
of wise and skilful people
who have the gift of healing,
and in your hands.

Lord Jesus, come to me this day and at this time,
and show me that your healing touch
has never lost its ancient power.
I ask this for your love's sake. (*Adapted from William Barclay*)

Lord of the Passion,
you accepted to share our suffering
to teach us about patience in human illness.
Be with me now, and all those who are undergoing
pain, illness and disease;
give us the comfort of knowing
that by nobly bearing our cross,
we will come to share your glory
in a kingdom where pain and tears
can hold no sway.

At the end of the day

May the Lord support us all the day long,
till the shades lengthen and the evening comes,
and the busy world is hushed,
and the fever of life is over,
and our work is done.
Then in his mercy
may he give us a safe lodging,
and a holy rest,
and peace at the last. Amen. (*Cardinal Newman*)

Save us, Lord, while we are awake;
protect us while we sleep;
that we may keep watch with Christ
and rest with him in peace. (*Compline*)

May the Lord grant us a quiet night,
and a perfect end. (*Compline*)

All shall be well,
And all shall be well,
And all manner of thing
Shall be well. (*Mother Julian of Norwich*)

SONGS HYMNS AND REFRAINS

1   **Abba Father**   *Ginny Vissing*

Abba, Father, send your Spirit.Glory, Jesus Christ. (2)

Glory, hallelujah, glory, Jesus Christ (2)

I will give you living water ...

If you seek me you will find me …

If you listen you will hear me...

Come, my children, I will teach you …

I'm your shepherd, I will lead you...

Peace I leave you, peace I give you...

I'm your life and resurrection...

Glory Father, glory Spirit...

2   **Adoramus Te**   *Taizé*

Adoramus Te Domine.

3   **All creatures of our God and King**   *William Henry Draper*

All creatures of our God and King,
lift up your voice and with us sing
alleluia, alleluia!
Thou burning sun with golden beam,
thou silver moon with softer gleam:

O praise him, O praise him,
alleluia, alleluia, alleluia.

Thou rushing wind that art so strong,
ye clouds that sail in heaven along,
O praise him, alleluia!
Thou rising morn, in praise rejoice,
ye lights of evening, find a voice:

Thou flowing water, pure and clear,
make music for thy Lord to hear,

alleluia, alleluia!
Thou fire so masterful and bright,
that givest us both warmth and light:

Dear mother earth, who day by day
unfoldest blessings on our way,
O praise him, alleluia!
The flowers and fruits that in thee grow
let them his glory also show:

And all who are of tender heart,
forgiving others, take your part,
O sing ye, alleluia!
Ye who long pain and sorrow bear,
praise God and on him cast your care:

And thou, most kind and gentle death,
waiting to hush our latest breath,
O praise him, alleluia!
Thou leadest home the child of God,
and Christ our Lord the way hath trod:

Let all things their Creator bless,
and worship him in humbleness,
O praise him, alleluia!
Praise, praise the Father, praise the Son,
and praise the Spirit, Three in One.

4   **All Hail to You, Mary**   *David Konstant*

All hail to you, Mary,
most favoured by God,
O teach us to follow
the path you once trod.

Ave, ave, ave Maria. (2)

When Gabriel had spoken
you humbly said "Yes".
May we have the courage
God's word to confess.

To those for whom sickness
and sadness are near,
show Jesus your first born,
our Saviour from fear.

With Joseph your husband
you cared for our Lord.
Guide parents and children
to life's one reward.

You treasured, dear mother,
the truth God revealed.
By seeking true wisdom
our faith will be sealed.

You spoke at the wedding
and Christ gave them wine.
He now gives his people
the true bread divine.

We trustfully echo
the prayer of your Son
that all of God's children
may love and be one.

In anguish enfolded
are mother and Son.
By sharing their passion
our victory is won.

When Christ died he gave you
as mankind's new Eve.
Inspire all your children
to love, hope, believe.

God's life was your living
with him you found peace.
May his loving presence
in us find increase.

5 All Over the World

Roy Turner

All over the world, the Spirit is moving.
all over the world,
as the prophets said it would be.
All over the world
there's a mighty revelation
of the glory of the Lord,
as the waters cover the sea.

All over the land…

All over the Church…

All over us all…

Deep down in our hearts…

6 All people that on earth do dwell

William Keithe

All people that on earth do dwell,
sing to the Lord with cheerful voice;
him serve with fear, his praise forth tell,
come ye before him and rejoice.

The Lord, ye know, is God indeed,
without our aid he did us make;
we are his folk, he doth us feed
and for his sheep he doth us take.

O enter then his gates with praise,
approach with joy his courts unto;
praise, laud, and bless his name always,
for it is seemly so to do.

For why? The Lord our God is good:
his mercy is for ever sure;
his truth at all times firmly stood,
and shall from age to age endure.

To Father, Son and Holy Ghost,
the God whom heaven and earth adore,
from men and from the angel-host
be praise and glory evermore.

7 All that I am
Sebastian Temple

All that I am, all that I do,
all that I'll ever have, I offer now to you.
Take and sanctify these gifts for your honour Lord.
Knowing that I love and serve you is enough reward.
All that I am, all that I do,
all that I'll ever have, I offer now to you.

All that I dream, all that I pray,
all that I'll ever make, I give to you today.
Take and sanctify these gifts for your honour Lord.
Knowing that I love and serve you is enough reward.
All that I am, all that I do,
all that I'll ever have, I offer now to you.

8 All ye who seek a comfort sure
tr. Edward Caswell

All ye who seek a comfort sure
in trouble and distress,
whatever sorrow vex the mind,
or guilt the soul oppress.

Jesus, who gave himself for you
upon the cross to die,
opens to you his sacred heart;
oh, to that heart draw nigh.

Ye hear how kindly he invites;
ye hear his words so blest:
'All ye that labour come to me,
and I will give you rest.'

Jesus, thou joy of saints on high,
thou hope of sinners here,
attracted by those loving words
to thee I lift my prayer.

Wash thou my wounds in that dear blood,
which forth from thee doth flow;
new grace, new hope inspire, a new
and better heart bestow.

9 Alleluia, alleluia, give thanks

Don Fishel

Alleluia, alleluia, give thanks to the risen Lord,
Alleluia, alleluia, give praise to his name.

Jesus is Lord of all the earth.
He is the king of creation.

Spread the good news o'er all the earth.
Jesus has died and is risen.

We have been crucified with Christ.
Now we shall live for ever.

God has proclaimed the just reward:
life for all men, alleluia.

Come, let us praise the living God,
joyfully sing to our Saviour.

10 Alleluia, sing to Jesus

W Chatterton Dix

Alleluia, sing to Jesus,
his the sceptre, his the throne;
alleluia, his the triumph,
his the victory alone:
hark! the songs of peaceful Sion
thunder like a mighty flood;
Jesus, out of every nation,
hath redeemed us by his blood.

Alleluia, not as orphans
are we left in sorrow now;
alleluia, he is near us,
faith believes, nor questions how;
though the cloud from sight received him
when the forty days were o'er,
shall our hearts forget his promise,
'I am with your evermore'?

Alleluia, Bread of Angels,
thou on earth our food our stay;
alleluia, here the sinful
flee to thee from day to day;

intercessor, friend of sinners,
earth's Redeemer, plead for me,
where the songs of all the sinless
sweep across the crystal sea.

Alleluia, King eternal
thee the Lord of lords we own;
alleluia, born of Mary,
earth thy footstool, heaven thy throne;
thou within the veil hast entered,
robed in flesh, our great High Priest;
thou on earth both priest and victim
in the Eucharistic Feast.

11 As I kneel before you   *Maria Parkinson*

As I kneel before you,
as I bow my head in prayer,
take this day, make it yours
and fill me with your love.

Ave, Maria gratia plena,
Dominus tecum, benedicta tu.

All I have I give you,
ev'ry dream and wish are yours.
Mother of Christ, Mother of mine,
present them to my Lord.

As I kneel before you,
and I see your smiling face,
ev'ry thought, ev'ry word
is lost in your embrace.

12 Awake from your slumber (City of God) *Daniel L Schutte*

Awake from your slumber! Arise from your sleep!
A new day is dawning for all those who weep.
The people in darkness have seen a great light.
The Lord of our longing has conquered the night.

Let us build the City of God.
May our tears be turned into dancing!
For the Lord our light and our love,
has turned the night into day.

We are sons of the morning;
we are daughters of day.
The One who has loved us has brightened our way.
The Lord of all kindness has called us to be
a light for his people to set their hearts free.

God is light; in him there is no darkness,
let us walk in his light, his children one and all.
O comfort my people; make gentle your words.
Proclaim to my city the day of her birth.
O city of gladness, now lift up your voice!
Proclaim the good tidings that all may rejoice!

13   **Be still and know that I am God**   *Anonymous*

Be still and know that I am God… (3)
I am the Lord that healeth thee… (3)
In thee, O Lord, I put my trust… (3)

14   **Be still, for the presence of the Lord**   *David J Evans*

Be still, for the presence of the Lord,
the Holy One is here.
Come bow before him now with reverence and fear.
In Him no sin is found,
we stand on holy ground.
Be still, for the presence of the Lord,
the Holy One is here.

Be still for the glory of the Lord
is shining all around;
He burns with holy fire,
with splendour he is crowned.
How awesome is the sight,
our radiant King of light.
Be still, for the glory of the Lord is shining all around.

Be still, for the power of the Lord
is moving in this place,
He comes to cleanse and heal, to minister his grace.
No work too hard for Him,
in faith receive from Him:
Be still, for the power of the Lord
is moving in this place.

15 **Because the Lord is my shepherd,** *Christopher Walker*

Because the Lord is my shepherd,
I have ev'rything I need.
He lets me rest in the meadow
and leads me to the quiet streams.
He restores my soul and leads me
in the paths that are right:

Lord, you are my shepherd, you are my friend.
I want to follow you always, just to
follow my friend.

And when the road leads to darkness,
I shall walk there unafraid.
Even when death is close
I have courage for your help is there.
You are close beside me with comfort,
you are guiding my way:

In love you make me a banquet
for my enemies to see.
You make me welcome, pouring down
honour from your mighty hand;
and this joy fills me with gladness,
it is too much to bear:

Your goodness always is with me
and your mercy I know.
Your loving kindness strengthens me
always as I go through life.
I shall dwell in your presence forever,
giving praise to your name:

16 Bind us together

Bob Gillman

Bind us together, Lord, bind us together
with cords that cannot be broken.
Bind us together, Lord, bind us together,
bind us together in love.

There is only one God,
there is only one King,
There is only one body,
that is why we sing.

Fit for the glory of God,
purchased by his precious blood,
born with the right to be free:
Jesus the victory has won.

We are the fam'ly of God,
we are his promise divine.
We are his chosen desire,
we are the glorious new wine.

17 Bless the Lord my soul

Taizé

Bless the Lord my soul,
and bless his holy name.
Bless the Lord my soul,
he rescues me from death.

18 Blest are you, Lord, God of all creation

Aniceto Nazareth

Blest are you, Lord, God of all creation,
thanks to your goodness this bread we offer:
fruit of the earth, work of our hands,
it will become the bread of life

Blessed be God! Blessed be God! Blessed be God forever! Amen!
Blessed be God! Blessed be God! Blessed be God forever! Amen!

Blest are you, Lord, God of all creation,
thanks to your goodness this wine we offer:
fruit of the earth, work of our hands,
it will become the cup of life.

19 Blest be the Lord

Daniel L Schutte

Blest be the Lord; blest be the Lord,
the God of mercy, the God who saves.
I shall not fear the dark of night,
nor the arrow that flies by day.

He will release me from the nets of all my foes.
He will protect me from their wicked hands.
Beneath the shadow of his wings I will rejoice
to find a dwelling place secure.

I need not shrink before the terrors of the night,
nor stand alone before the light of day.
No harm shall come to me, no arrow strike me down,
no evil settle in my soul.

Although a thousand strong have fallen at my side,
I'll not be shaken with the Lord at hand.
His faithful love is all the armour that I need
to wage my battle with the foe.

20 Colours of day

Sue McClellan, John Pac & Keith Ryecroft

Colours of day dawn into the mind,
the sun has come up, the night is behind.
Go down in the city, into the street,
and let's give the message to the people we meet.

So light up the fire and let the flame burn,
open the door, let Jesus return.
Take seeds of his Spirit, let the fruit grow,
tell the people of Jesus, let his love show.

Go through the park, on into the town;
the sun still shines on it; never goes down.
The light of the world is risen again;
the people of darkness are needing our friend.

Open your eyes, look into the sky,
the darkness has come the sun came to die.
The evening draws on, the sun disappears,
but Jesus is living, and his Spirit is near.

21 Come and go with me

Anonymous

Come and go with me to my Father's house,
to my Father's house, to my Father's house.
Come and go with me to my Father's house,
Where there's joy, joy, joy.

It's not very far to my Father's house…

There is room for all in my Father's house…

Everything is free in my Father's house…

Jesus is the way to my Father's house…

Jesus is the light in my Father's house…

We will praise the Lord in my Father's house…

22 Come and praise

A Carter

Come and praise him, royal priesthood.
Come and worship, holy nation.
Worship Jesus, our redeemer.
He is precious, King of glory.

23 Come back to me

Gregory Norbert

Come back to me with all your heart.
Don't let fear keep us apart.
Trees do bend, though straight and tall;
so must we to others call.

*Long have I waited for your
coming home to me and living deeply our new life.*

The wilderness will lead you,
to your heart where I will speak.
Integrity and justice with tenderness
you shall know.

You shall sleep secure with peace;
faithfulness will be your joy.
Long have I waited for your coming home to me
and living deeply our new life.

Come back to me with all your heart.
Don't let fear keep us apart.
Trees do bend, though straight and tall;
so must we to others' call.

24 Come, Holy Ghost, Creator, come *ascr. to Rabanus Marus*

Come, Holy Ghost, Creator, come
from thy bright heavenly throne,
come, take possession of our souls,
and make them all thine own.

Thou who art called the Paraclete,
best gift of God above,
the living spring, the living fire,
sweet unction and true love.

Thou who are sev'nfold in thy grace,
finger of God's right hand;
his promise, teaching little ones
to speak and understand.

O guide our minds with thy blest light,
with love our hearts inflame;
and with thy strength, which ne'er decays,
confirm our mortal frame.

Far from us drive our deadly foe;
true peace unto us bring;
and through all perils lead us safe
beneath thy sacred wing.

Through thee may we the Father know,
through thee the eternal Son,
and thee the Spirit of them both,
thrice-blessed Three in One.

All glory to the Father be,
with his co-equal Son:
the same to thee, great Paraclete,
while endless ages run.

25 Come, Lord Jesus, come

Kevin Mayhew

Come, Lord Jesus, come.
Come, take my hands, take them for your work.
Take them for your service, Lord.
Take them for your glory, Lord.
Come, Lord Jesus, come.
Come, Lord Jesus, take my hands.

Come, Lord Jesus, come.
Come, take my eyes, may they shine with joy.
Take them for your service, Lord.
Take them for your glory, Lord.
Come, Lord Jesus, come.
Come, Lord Jesus, take my eyes.

Come, Lord Jesus, come
Come, take my lips, may they speak your truth.
Take them for your service, Lord.
Take them for your glory, Lord.
Come, Lord Jesus, come.
Come, Lord Jesus, take my lips.

Come, Lord Jesus, come.
Come take my feet, may they walk your path.
Take them for your service, Lord.
Take them for your glory, Lord.
Come, Lord Jesus, come.
Come, Lord Jesus, take my feet.

Come, Lord Jesus, come.
Come, take my heart, fill it with your love.
Take it for your service, Lord.
Take it for your glory, Lord.
Come, Lord Jesus, come.
Come, Lord Jesus, take my heart.

Come, Lord Jesus, come.
Come, take my life, take it for your own.
Take it for your service, Lord.
Take it for your glory, Lord.
Come, Lord Jesus, come.
Come, Lord Jesus, take my life.

26   Dear Lord and Father of mankind

J. G. Whittier

Dear Lord and Father of mankind,
forgive our foolish ways!
Re-clothe us in our rightful mind,
in purer lives thy service find,
in deeper rev'rence praise. (2)

In simple trust like theirs who heard,
beside the Syrian sea,
the gracious calling of the Lord,
let us, like them, without a word,
rise up and follow thee. (2)

O Sabbath rest by Galilee!
O calm of hills above,
where Jesus knelt to share with thee
the silence of eternity,
interpreted by love! (2)

Drop thy still dews of quietness,
till all our strivings cease;
take from our souls the strain and stress,
and let ordered lives confess
the beauty of thy peace. (2)

Breath through the heats of our desire
thy coolness and thy balm;
let sense be dumb, let flesh retire;
speak through the earthquake, wind and fire,
O still small voice of calm! (2)

27   Do not be afraid

Gerald Markland

Do not be afraid, for I have redeemed you.
I have called you by your name; you are mine.

When you walk through the waters I'll be with you.
You will never sink beneath the waves.

When the fire is burning all around you,
you will never be consumed by the flames.

When the fear of loneliness is looming,
then remember I am at your side.

When you dwell in the exile of the stranger,
remember you are precious in my eyes.

You are mine, O my child, I am your Father,
and I love you with a perfect love.

28 Eat this bread
Taizé

Eat this bread, drink this cup,
come to me and never be hungry.
Eat this bread, drink this cup,
trust in me and you will not thirst.

29 Father, I place Into Your hands
J. Hewer

Father, I place into your hands
the things that I can't do.
Father, I place into your hands
the times that I've been through.
Father, I place into your hands
the way that I should go,
for I know I always can trust you.

Father, I place into your hands
my friends and family.
Father, I place into your hands
the things that trouble me.
Father, I place into your hands
the person I would be,
for I know I always can trust you.

Father, we love to see your face,
we love to hear your voice.
Father, we love to sing your praise,
and in your name rejoice.
Father, we love to walk with you
and in your presence rest,
for we know we always can trust you.

Father, I want to be with you
and do the things you do.
Father, I want to speak the words
that you are speaking too.
Father, I want to love the ones
that you will draw to you,
for I know that I am one with you.

30 Father in my life I see

Frank Anderson MSC

Father, in my life I see,
you are God, who walks with me.
You hold my life in your hands:
close beside you I will stand.
I give all my life to you:
help me, Father, to be true.

Jesus, in my life I see …

Spirit, in my life I see …

31 Father, we adore you

Tony Coelho

Father, we adore you,
lay our lives before you.
How we love you.

Jesus, we adore you …

Spirit, we adore you …

32 Father, we love you, we praise you

Donna Adkins

Father, we love you, we praise you, we adore you.
Glorify your name in all the earth!
Glorify your name, glorify your name,
glorify your name in all the earth!

Jesus, we love you, we praise you, we adore you …

Spirit, we love you, we praise you, we adore you …

33 Follow me, follow me

Michael Cockett

Follow me, follow me, leave your home and family,
leave your fishing nets and boats upon the shore.
Leave the seed that you have sown,
leave the crops that you've grown,
leave the people you have known and follow me.

The foxes have their holes
and the swallows have their nests,
but the Son of man has no place to lay down.
I do not offer comfort, I do not offer wealth,
but in me will all happiness be found.

If you would follow me,
you must leave old ways behind.
You must take my cross and follow on my path.
You may be far from loved ones,
you may be far from home,
but my Father will welcome you at last.

Although I go away you will never be alone,
for the Spirit will be there to comfort you.
Though all of you may scatter,
each follow his own path,
still the Spirit of love will lead you home.

HYMNS

34 For all the saints

W. Walsham How

For all the saints who from their labours rest,
who thee by faith before the world confest,
thy name, O Jesus be for every blest.

Alleluia! Alleluia!

Thou wast their rock, their fortress, and their might;
thou, Lord, their captain in the well-fought fight;
thou in the darkness drear their one true light.

O may thy soldiers, faithful, true and bold,
fight as the saints who nobly fought of old,
and win, with them, the victor's crown of gold.

O blest communion! fellowship divine!
We feebly struggle, they in glory shine;
yet all are one in thee, for all are thine.

And when the strife is fierce, the warfare long,
steals on the ear the distant triumph-song,
and hearts are brave again, and arms are strong.

The golden evening brightens in the west;
soon, soon to faithful warriors cometh rest:
sweet is the calm of paradise the blest.

But lo! there breaks a yet more glorious day;
the saints triumphant rise in bright array:
the king of glory passes on his way.

From earth's wide bounds, from ocean's farthest coast,
through gates of pearl streams in the countless host,
singing to Father, Son and Holy Ghost.

35 For You are my God   *John Foley SJ*

For you are my God, you alone are my joy.
Defend me, O Lord.

You give marvellous comrades to me:
the faithful who dwell in your land.
Those who choose alien gods
have chosen an alien band.

You are my portion and cup;
it is you that I claim for my prize.
Your heritage is my delight,
the lot you have given to me.

Glad are my heart and my soul;
securely my body shall rest.
For you will not leave me for dead,
nor lead your beloved astray.

You show me the path for my life;
in your presence the fullness of joy.
To be at your right hand for ever
for me would be happiness always.

36 From heaven You came (Servant King) *Graham Kendrick*

From heaven You came, helpless babe,
entered our world, Your glory veiled,
not to be served but to serve,
and give Your life that we might live.

This is our God, the Servant King,
He calls us now to follow Him,
to bring our lives as a daily offering
of worship to the Servant King.

There in the garden of tears
my heavy load He chose to bear;
His heart with sorrow was torn,
'Yet not my will but yours,' He said.

Come see His hands and His feet,
the scars that speak of the sacrifice,
hands that flung stars into space
to cruel nails surrendered.

So let us learn how to serve
and in our lives enthrone Him,
each other's needs to prefer,
for it is Christ we're serving.

37 Gifts of bread and wine *Christine McCann*

Gifts of bread and wine, gifts we've offered,
fruits of labour, fruits of love;
taken, offered, sanctified,
blessed and broken; words of one who died:

'Take my body, take my saving blood.'
Gifts of bread and wine: Christ our Lord.

Christ our Saviour, living presence here
as he promised while on earth:
'I am with you for all time,
I am with you in this bread and wine.'

Through the Father, with the Spirit,
one in union with the Son,
for God's people, joined in prayer,
faith is strengthened by the food we share.

38 Give me joy

Traditional

Give me joy in my heart, keep me praising.
Give me joy in my heart I pray.
Give me joy in my heart, keep me praising.
Keep me praising till the end of day.

Sing Hosanna! Sing Hosanna!
Sing Hosanna to the King of Kings!
Sing Hosanna! Sing Hosanna!
Sing Hosanna to the King!

Give me peace in my heart, keep me resting …

Give me love in my heart, keep me serving …

Give me oil in my lamp, keep me burning …

39 Glory and praise to our God

Daniel L Schutte

Glory and praise to our God,
who alone gives light to our days.
Many are the blessings he bears
to those who trust in his ways.

We the daughters and sons of him
who built the valleys and plains,
praise the wonders our God has done
in every heart that sings.

In his wisdom he strengthens us
like gold that's tested in fire.
Though the power of sin prevails,
our God is there to save.

Ev'ry moment of ev'ry day
our God is waiting to save,
always ready to seek the lost,
to answer those who pray.

God has watered our barren land
and spent his merciful rain.
Now the rivers of life run full
for anyone to drink.

40 Go, the Mass is ended

Sr. Marie Lydia Pereira

Go, the Mass is ended, children of the Lord.
Take his word to others
as you've heard it spoken to you.
Go, the Mass is ended, go and tell the world
the Lord is good, the Lord is kind,
and loves us ev'ry one.

Go, the Mass is ended, take his love to all.
Gladden all who meet you,
fill their hearts with hope and courage.
Go, the Mass is ended, fill the world with love,
and give to all what you've received -
the peace and joy of Christ.

Go, the Mass is ended, strengthened in the Lord,
lighten ev'ry burden,
spread the joy of Christ around you.
Go, the Mass is ended, take his peace to all.
This day is yours to change the world -
to make God known and loved.

41 God forgave my sin (Freely, freely)

Carol Owens

God forgave my sin in Jesus' name.
I've been born again in Jesus' name.
And in Jesus' name I come to you
to share his love as he told me to.

He said: 'Freely, freely you have received;
freely, freely give.
Go in my name, and because you believe,
others will know that I live.'

All pow'r is giv'n in Jesus' name,
in earth and heav'n in Jesus' name.
And in Jesus' name I come to you
to share his pow'r as he told me to.

God gives us life in Jesus' name,
he lives in us in Jesus' name;
and in Jesus' name I come to you
to share his peace as he told me to.

42 God has gladdened my heart (Lourdes Magnificat)

God has gladdened my heart with joy, alleluia!
He has vested me with holiness, alleluia!

Sing my soul of the glory of the Lord;
with God's Spirit I'm full to overflowing!

See the love that God showers on the poor:
see the Lord overshadow those who fear him.

All the world will join in this song of praise,
for through me they now know the Lord is with them.

To fulfil what he promised from of old
God has chosen me! Bless his name for ever.

Day by day, year by year, God's love is sure;
those who listen and keep his word will know it.

See the pow'r of the Lord destroy the strong!
Those who think themselves strong, the Lord will humble.

Empty pride, self conceit, the Lord ignores;
but he raises the poor who call upon him.

No more thirst, no more hunger with the Lord;
unsurpassed in his goodness to his people.

See the care that the Lord shows to us all.
Day by day, year by year, God's love unending.

Praise the Father, the Son, the Spirit, praise!
May the glory of God be sung for ever.

43 Guide me, O thou great Redeemer   *W Williams*

Guide me, O thou great Redeemer,
pilgrim through this barren land;
I am weak, but thou art mighty,
hold me with thy pow'rful hand:
bread of heaven, bread of heaven,
feed me till I want no more.(2)

Open now the crystal fountain,
whence the healing stream doth flow;
let the fire and cloudy pillar

lead me all my journey through;
strong deliverer, strong deliverer
be thou still my strength and shield. (2)

When I tread the verge of Jordan,
bid my anxious fears subside,
death of death, and hell's destruction,
land me safe on Canaan's side;
songs of praises, songs of praises
I will ever give to thee.(2)

44   Hail, Queen of heav'n   *John Lingard*

Hail, Queen of heav'n, the ocean star,
guide of the wand'rer here below,
Thrown on life's surge, we claim thy care;
save us from peril and from woe.
Mother of Christ, star of the sea,
pray for the wand'rer, pray for me.

O gentle, chaste and spotless maid,
we sinners make our prayers through thee;
remind thy son that he has paid
the price of our iniquity.
Virgin most pure, star of the sea,
pray for the sinner, pray for me

Sojourners in this vale of tears,
to thee, blest advocate, we cry;
pity our sorrows, calm our fears,
and soothe with hope our misery.
Refuge in grief, star of the sea,
pray for the mourner, pray for me.

And while to him who reigns above,
in Godhead One, in Persons Three,
the source of life, of grace, of love,
homage we pay on bended knee
Do thou, bright Queen, star of the sea,
pray for thy children, pray for me.

45 Hail, Redeemer, King divine

Patrick Brennan

Hail, Redeemer, King divine!
Priest and Lamb, the throne is thine;
King, whose reign shall never cease,
Prince of everlasting peace.

Angels saints and nations sing:
'Praised be Jesus Christ, our King;
Lord of life, earth, sky and sea,
King of love on Calvary.'

King whose name creation thrills,
rule our minds, our hearts, our wills,
till in peace each nation rings
with thy praises, King of Kings.

King most holy, King of truth,
guide the lowly, guide the youth;
Christ thou King of glory bright,
be to us eternal light.

Shepherd-King, o'er mountains steep,
homeward bring the wandering sheep,
shelter in one royal fold
states and kingdoms, new and old.

46 He is Lord

Anonymous

He is Lord, He is Lord.
He is risen from the dead and he is Lord.
Ev'ry knee shall bow, ev'ry tongue confess
that Jesus Christ is Lord.

He is King …

He is Love …

47 Here in this place (Gather us in)

Marty Haugen

Here in this place, new light is streaming,
now is the darkness vanished away.
See, in this space, our fears and our dreamings,
brought here to you in the light of this day.

Gather us in the lost and forsaken,
gather us in the blind and the lame;
Call to us now, and we shall awaken,
we shall arise at the sound of our name.

We are the young our lives are a myst'ry
we are the old who yearn for your face.
We have been sung throughout all of hist'ry,
called to be light to the whole human race.
Gather us in the rich and the haughty,
gather us in the proud and the strong;
Give us a heart so meek and so lowly,
give us the courage to enter the song.

Here we will take the wine and the water,
here we will take the bread of new birth.
Here you shall call your sons and your daughters,
call us anew to be salt for the earth.
Give us to drink the wine of compassion,
give us to eat the bread that is you;
Nourish us well, and teach us to fashion,
lives that are holy and hearts that are true.

Not in the dark of buildings confining,
not in some heaven, light years away,
but here in this place, the new light is shining,
now is the Kingdom, now is the day.
Gather us in and hold us for ever,
gather us in and make us your own;
Gather us in all peoples together,
fire of love in our flesh and our bone.

48   He's got the whole world   *Traditional*

He's got the whole world in his hand.
He's got the whole wide world in his hand.
He's got the whole world in his hand.
He's got the whole world in his hand.

He's got you and me, brother, in his hand …

He's got you and me, sister, in his hand ...
He's got everybody here in his hand ...
He's got the whole world in his hand ...

49 Holy God, we praise thy name

C A Walworth

Holy God, we praise thy name;
Lord of all, we bow before thee!
All on earth thy sceptre own,
all in heaven above adore thee.
Infinite thy vast domain,
everlasting is thy reign.

Hark! The loud celestial hymn,
angel choirs above are raising;
cherubim and seraphim,
in unceasing chorus praising,
fill the heavens with sweet accord,
holy, holy, holy Lord.

Holy Father, holy Son,
Holy Spirit, three we name thee,
while in essence only one
undivided God we claim thee;
and adoring bend the knee
while we own the mystery.

Spare thy people, Lord, we pray,
by a thousand snares surrounded;
keep us without sin today;
never let us be confounded.
Lo, I put my trust in thee,
never, Lord, abandon me.

50 Holy Spirit of Fire

John Glynn

Holy Spirit of fire, flame everlasting,
so bright and clear,
speak this day in our hearts.
Lighten our darkness and purge us of fear,
Holy Spirit of fire.

The wind can blow or be still,
or water be parched by the sun.
A fire can die into dust:
But here the eternal Spirit of God
tells us a new world's begun.

Holy Spirit of love,
strong are the faithful who trust your pow'r.
Love who conquer our will,
teach us the words of the gospel of peace,
Holy Spirit of love.

Holy Spirit of God,
flame everlasting so bright and clear,
speak this day in our hearts.
Lighten our darkness and purge us of fear,
Holy Spirit of God

51   **Holy Virgin, by God's decree**   *J.P. Léçot tr. Raymond Lawrence*

Holy Virgin, by God's decree,
you were called eternally;
that he could give his Son to our race.
Mary, we praise you, hail, full of grace.

Ave, ave, ave, Maria.

By your faith and loving accord,
as the handmaid of the Lord,
you undertook God's plan to embrace,
Mary, we thank you, hail, full of grace.

Refuge for your children so weak,
sure protection all can seek.
Problems of life you help us to face.
Mary, we trust you, hail, full of grace.

To our needy world of today
love and beauty you portray,
showing the path to Christ we must trace.
Mary, our mother, hail, full of grace.

52   How great is our God

Author unknown

How great is our God, how great is his name!
How great is our God, for ever the same!

He rolled back the waters of the mighty Red Sea.
And he said: 'I'll never leave you.
Put your trust in me.'

He sent his Son, Jesus, to set us all free.
And he said: 'I'll never leave you.
Put your trust in me.'

He gave us his Spirit, and now we can see.
And he said: 'I'll never leave you.
Put your trust in me.'

53   How lovely on the mountains

Leonard. E. Smith Jnr

How lovely on the mountains are the feet of him
who brings good news, good news,
announcing peace, proclaiming news of happiness:

Our God reigns (6)

You watchmen, lift your voices joyfully as one,
shout for your king, your king!
See eye to eye, the Lord restoring Sion:

Wasteplaces of Jerusalem, break forth with joy!
We are redeemed, redeemed.
The Lord has saved and comforted his people.

Ends of the earth, see the salvation of our God!
Jesus is Lord, is Lord!
Before the nations, he has bared his holy arm.

54   I am the bread of life

Suzanne Toolan

I am the Bread of life.
You who come to me shall not hunger;
and who believe in me shall not thirst.
No-one can come to me
unless the Father beckons.

And I will raise you up, and I will raise you up,
and I will raise you up on the last day.

The bread that I will give
is my flesh for the life of the world,
and if you eat of this bread,
you shall live forever, you shall live forever.

Unless you eat of the flesh of the Son of Man
and drink of his blood, and drink of his blood,
you shall not have life within you.

I am the Resurrection, I am the life.
If you believe in me, even though you die,
you shall live forever.

Yes, Lord, I believe that you are the Christ,
the Son of God, who have come,
Into the world.

55 I danced in the morning
Sydney Carter

I danced in the morning when the world was begun
and I danced in the moon and the stars and the sun,
and I came down from heaven
and I danced on the earth,
at Bethlehem I had my birth.

Dance, then, wherever you may be
I am the Lord of the Dance, said he,
And I'll lead you all wherever you may be,
And I'll lead you all in the dance, said he.

I danced for the scribe and the Pharisee
but they would not dance
and they wouldn't follow me,
I danced for the fishermen, for James and John;
they came with me and the dance went on.

I danced on the Sabbath and I cured the lame.
The holy people said it was a shame.
They whipped and they stripped
and they hung me on high,
and they left me there on the cross to die.

I danced on a Friday when the sky turned black.
It's hard to dance with the devil on your back.
They buried my body and they thought I'd gone,
but I am the dance and I still go on.

They cut me down and I leapt up high.
I am the life that'll never, never die,
I'll live in you if you'll live in me,
I am the Lord of the Dance, said he.

56 I give my hands

I give my hands to do your work
and, Jesus Lord, I give them willingly.
I give my feet to go your way
and every step I shall take cheerfully.

O, the joy of the Lord is my strength, my strength!
O, the joy of the Lord is my help, my help!
For the pow'r of his Spirit is in my soul
and the joy of the Lord is my strength.

I give my eyes to see the world
and every one, in just the way you do.
I give my tongue to speak your words,
to spread your name and freedom giving truth.

I give my mind in every way
so that each thought I have will come from you.
I give my spirit to you, Lord,
and every day my prayer will spring anew.

I give my heart that you may love
in me your Father and the human race.
I give myself that you may grow
in me and make my life a song of praise.

57 I'll sing a hymn to Mary

John Wyse

I'll sing a hymn to Mary,
the mother of my God,
the Virgin of all virgins,
of David's royal blood.

O teach me, Holy Mary,
a loving song to frame,
when wicked men blaspheme thee,
to love and bless thy name.

O noble Tower of David,
of gold and ivory,
the Ark of God's own promise,
the gate of heav'n to me,
to live and not to love thee,
would fill my soul with shame;
when wicked men blaspheme thee,
I'll love and bless thy name.

The Saints are high in glory,
with golden crowns so bright;
but brighter far is Mary,
upon her throne of light.
O that which God did give thee,
let mortal ne'er disclaim;
when wicked men blaspheme thee,
I'll love and bless thy name.

But in the crown of Mary,
there lies a wondrous gem,
as Queen of all the Angels,
which Mary shares with them:
no sin hath e'er defiled thee,
so doth our faith proclaim;
when wicked men blaspheme thee,
I'll love and bless thy name.

58   I, the Lord of sea and sky   *Daniel L Schutte*

I, the Lord of sea and sky,
I have heard my people cry.
All who dwell in dark and sin,
my hand will save.
I who made the stars of night,
I will make their darkness bright.

Who will bear my light to them?
Whom shall I send?

Here I am, Lord. Is it I Lord?
I have heard you calling in the night.
I will go, Lord, if you lead me.
I will hold your people in my heart.

I, the Lord of snow and rain,
I have borne my people's pain.
I have wept for love of them.
They turn away.
I will break their hearts of stone,
give them hearts for love alone.
I will speak my word to them.
Whom shall I send?

I, the Lord of wind and flame,
I will tend the poor and lame.
I will set a feast for them.
My hand will save.
Finest bread I will provide
till their hearts be satisfied.
I will give my life to them.
Whom shall I send?

59   I watch the sunrise

John Glynn

I watch the sunrise lighting the sky,
casting its shadows near.
And on this morning, bright though it be,
I feel those shadows near me.

But you are always close to me,
following all my ways.
May I be always close to you,
following all your ways, Lord.

I watch the sunlight shine through the clouds,
warming the earth below.
And at the mid-day, life seems to say:
"I feel your brightness near me."

For you are always close to me...

I watch the sunset fading away,
lighting the clouds with sleep.
And as the evening closes its eyes,
I feel your presence near me.

For you are always close to me

I watch the moonlight guarding the night,
waiting till morning comes.
The air is silent, earth is at rest -
only your peace is near me.

Yes, you are always close to me...

60 I will be with you

Gerald Markland

I will be with you wherever you go.
Go now throughout the world!
I will be with you in all that you say.
Go now and spread my word!

Come, walk with me on stormy waters.
Why fear? Reach out, and I'll be there.

And you, my friend, will you now leave me,
or do you know me as your Lord?

Your life will be transformed with power
by living truly in my name.

And if you say· 'Yes, Lord, I love you,'
then feed my lambs and feed my sheep.

61 I will never forget you, my people

Carey Landry

I will never forget you, my people;
I have carved you on the palm of my hand.
I will never forget you; I will not leave you orphaned.
I will never forget my own.

Does a mother forget her baby?
Or a woman the child within her womb?
Yet even if these forget, yes, even if these forget,
I will never forget my own.

I will never forget you, my people;
I have carved you on the palm of my hand.
I will never forget you; I will not leave you orphaned.
I will never forget my own.

62   I will sing, I will sing

Max Dyer

I will sing, I will sing a song unto the Lord. (3)
Alleluia, glory to the Lord.

Allelu, alleluia, glory to the Lord. (3)
Alleluia, glory to the Lord.

We will come, we will come
as one before the Lord. (3)
Alleluia, glory to the Lord.

If the Son, if the Son shall make you free, (3)
you shall be free indeed.

They that sow in tears shall reap in joy. (3)
Alleluia, glory to the Lord.

Ev'ry knee shall bow and ev'ry tongue confess (3)
that Jesus Christ is Lord.

In his name, in his name we have the victory. (3)
Alleluia, glory to the Lord.

63   If God is for us

John B Foley

If God is for us, who can be against,
if the Spirit of God has set us free? (2)

I know that nothing in this world
can ever take us from his love.

Nothing can take us from his love,
poured out in Jesus, the Lord.

And nothing present or to come
can ever take us from his love.

I know that neither death nor life
can ever take us from his love.

64 Immaculate Mary (Lourdes Hymn)   *Anonymous*

Immaculate Mary!
Our hearts are on fire,
that title so wondrous
fills all our desire.

Ave, ave, ave Maria!
Ave, ave, ave Maria!

We pray for God's glory,
may his Kingdom come!
We pray for his vicar,
our father, and Rome.

We pray for our mother
the Church upon earth,
and bless, sweetest Lady,
the land of our birth.

For poor, sick, afflicted
thy mercy we crave;
and comfort the dying
thou light of the grave.

There is no need, Mary,
nor ever has been,
which thou canst not succour,
Immaculate Queen.

In grief and temptation,
in joy or in pain,
we'll ask thee, our mother,
nor seek thee in vain.

O bless us, dear Lady,
with blessings from heaven.
And to our petitions
let answer be given.

In death's solemn moment,
our mother, be nigh;
as children of Mary-
O teach us to die.

And crown thy sweet mercy
with this special grace,
to behold soon in heaven
God's ravishing face.

To God be all glory
and worship for aye,
and to God's virgin mother
an endless Ave.

65   In bread we bring you, Lord   *Kevin Nichols*

In bread we bring you, Lord, our bodies' labour.
In wine we offer you our spirits' grief,
We do not ask you, Lord, who is my neighbour?
but stand united now, one in belief.
Oh we have gladly heard your Word your holy Word,
and now in answer, Lord, our gifts we bring.
Our selfish hearts make true, our failing faith renew,
our lives belong to you, our Lord and King.

The bread we offer you is blessed and broken,
and it becomes for us our spirit's food.
Over the cup we bring your word is spoken;
make it your gift to us, your healing blood.
Take all that daily toil plants in our heart's poor soil,
take all we start and spoil, each hopeful dream,
the chances we have missed, the graces we resist,
Lord, in thy Eucharist, take and redeem.

66   In the love of God and neighbour   *Estelle White*

In the love of God and neighbour,
we are gathered at his table:
gifts of bread and wine
will become a sign
of the love our Father gave us
through the Son who came to save us
by the Spirit blest.

So we offer our tomorrows,
all our present joys and sorrows,
every heart and will,
talents, gifts and skills.
For the riches we've been given
to the Trinity of heaven
we give thanks and praise.

67 Jesus is the Bread of Life (His Banner over me)

Jesus is the Bread of Life
and His banner over me is love;
Jesus is the Bread of Life
and His banner over me is love;
Jesus is the Bread of Life
and His banner over me is love;
His banner over me is love.

He brings us to his banqueting table …

The one way to peace is the power of the cross …

We gather as one and we join hands together …

He calls us all to go forth and witness …

68 Jesus, my Lord, my God, my all   *Frederick William Faber*

Jesus, my Lord, my God, my all,
how can I love thee as I ought?
And how revere this wondrous gift,
so far surpassing hope or thought?

Sweet Sacrament, we thee adore;
Oh, make us love thee more and more.

Had I but Mary's sinless heart
to love thee with, my dearest King,
Oh, with what bursts of fervent praise
thy goodness, Jesus, would I sing!

Ah, see! within a creature's hand
the vast Creator deigns to be,
reposing, infant-like, as though
on Joseph's arm, or Mary's knee.

Thy body, soul, and Godhead, all;
O mystery of love divine!
I cannot compass all I have,
for all thou hast and art are mine.

Sound, sound, his praises higher still
and come ye angels to our aid,
'tis God, 'tis God, the very God
whose praise both men and angels made.

69 Jesus, remember me

Taizé

Jesus, remember me,
when you come into your Kingdom,
Jesus, remember me,
when you come into your Kingdom.

70 Laudate Dominum

Taizé

Laudate Dominum,
Laudate Dominum omnes gentes.
Alleluia.

71 Lay your hands gently upon us

Carey Landry

Lay your hands gently upon us,
let their touch render your peace,
let them bring your forgiveness and healing,
lay your hands, gently lay your hands.

You were sent to free the broken-hearted.
You were sent to give sight to the blind.
You desire to heal all our illness.
Lay your hands, gently lay your hands.

Lord, we come to you through one another,
Lord, we come to you in all our need.
Lord, we come to you seeking wholeness.
Lay your hands, gently lay your hands.

72   Lead, kindly light

John Henry Newman

Lead, kindly light amid th' encircling gloom,
lead thou me on;
the night is dark, and I am far from home,
lead thou me on.
Keep thou my feet; I do not ask to see
the distant scene; one step enough for me.

I was not ever thus, nor prayed that thou shouldst
lead me on;
I loved to chose and see my path; but now
lead thou me on.
I loved the garish day, and, spite of fears,
pride ruled my will; remember not past years.

So long thy power hath blest me, sure it still
will lead me on
o'er moor and fen, o'er crag and torrent, till the night
is gone,
and with the morn those angels faces smile
which I have loved long since, and lost awhile.

73   Let there be love

Dave Bilbrough

Let there be love shared among us,
let there be love in our eyes.
May now your love sweep this nation;
cause us, O Lord ,to arise.
Give us a fresh understanding,
filled with your love that is real,
let there be love shared among us, let there be love.

Let there be peace shared among us ...

Let there be hope shared among us ...

Let there be joy shared among us ...

Let there be trust shared among us ...

Let there be love shared among us ...

74 Like a shepherd

Bob Dufford

Like a shepherd he feeds his flock
and gathers the lambs in his arms,
holding them carefully, close to his heart,
leading them home.

Say to the cities of Judah:
'Prepare the way of the Lord.'
Go to the mountain top, lift your voice;
Jerusalem, here is your God.

I myself will shepherd them,
for others have led them astray.
The lost I will rescue and heal their wounds
and pasture them, giving them rest.

Come unto me if you are heavily burdened,
and take my yoke upon your shoulders.
I will give you rest.

75 Lord of all hopefulness

Jan Struther

Lord of all hopefulness,
Lord of all joy,
whose trust, ever child-like,
no cares could destroy,
be there at our waking,
and give us, we pray,
your bliss in our hearts, Lord,
at the break of the day.

Lord of all eagerness,
Lord of all faith,
whose strong hands were skilled
at the plane and the lathe,
be there at our labours
and give us, we pray,
your strength in our hearts, Lord,
at the noon of the day.

Lord of all kindliness
Lord of all grace,
your hands swift to welcome,
your arms to embrace,
be there at our homing,
and give us, we pray,
your love in our hearts, Lord,
at the eve of the day.

Lord of all gentleness,
Lord of all calm,
whose voice is contentment,
whose presence is balm,
be there at our sleeping,
and give us, we pray,
your peace in our hearts, Lord,
at the end of the day.

76   Lord, Jesus Christ, you have come to us   *Patrick Appleford*

Lord, Jesus Christ,
you have come to us,
you are one with us, Mary's son.
Cleansing our souls from all their sin,
pouring your love and goodness in,
Jesus our love for you we sing,
living Lord.

Lord Jesus Christ,
now and ev'ry day
teach us how to pray, Son of God.
You have commanded us to do
this in remembrance, Lord, of you.
Into our lives your pow'r breaks through,
living Lord.

Lord Jesus Christ,
you have come to us,
born as one of us, Mary's Son.
Led out to die on Calvary,

risen from death to set us free,
living Lord Jesus, help us see
you are Lord.

Lord Jesus Christ,
I would come to you,
live my life for you, Son of God.
All your commands I know are true,
your many gifts will make me new,
into my life your pow'r breaks through,
living Lord.

77   Lord, the Light of Your Love   *Graham Kendrick*

Lord, the light of your love is shining
in the midst of the darkness, shining;
Jesus, Light of the World, shine upon us,
set us free by the truth You now bring us,
shine on me, shine on me.

Shine, Jesus, shine,
fill this land with the Father's glory:
blaze, Spirit, blaze
set our hearts on fire!
Flow, river, flow,
flood the nations with grace and mercy;
send forth Your word, Lord,
and let there be light!

Lord, I come to Your awesome presence,
from the shadows into Your radiance;
by the blood I may enter Your brightness.
search me, try me, consume all my darkness.
Shine on me, shine on me.

As we gaze on Your kingly brightness
so our faces display Your likeness,
ever changing from glory to glory,
mirrored here may our lives tell Your story.
Shine on me, shine on me.

78   Lord, you have come to the seashore

C Gabaráin

Lord, you have come to the seashore,
neither searching for the rich nor the wise,
desiring only that I should follow.

O, Lord, with your eyes set upon me,
gently smiling you have spoken my name;
all I longed for I have found by the water,
at your side, I will seek other shores.

Lord, see my goods, my possessions;
in my boat you find no power, no wealth.
Will you accept, then, my nets and labour?

Lord, take my hands and direct them.
Help me spend myself in seeking the lost,
returning love for the love you gave me.

Lord, as I drift on the waters,
be the resting place of my restless heart,
my life's companion, my friend and refuge.

79   Maiden yet a mother

Dante Alighieri tr. R. A. Knox

Maiden, yet a mother,
daughter of thy Son,
high beyond all other,
lowlier is none;
thou the consummation
planning by God's decree,
when our lost creation
nobler rose in thee!

Thus his day prepared,
he who all things made
'mid his creatures tarried,
in thy bosom laid;
there his love he nourished,
warmth that gave increase
to the root whence flourished
our eternal peace.

Noon on Sion's mountain
is thy charity;
hope its living fountain
finds, on earth, in thee:
lady, such thy power,
he, who grace would buy
not as of thy dower,
without wings would fly.

80 Majesty, worship His majesty

Jack W. Hayford

Majesty, worship His majesty;
unto Jesus be glory, honour and praise.
Majesty, kingdom, authority
flow from His throne unto His own: His anthem raise.
So exault, lift up on high the name of Jesus;
magnify, come glorify Christ Jesus the King.
Majesty, worship His majesty,
Jesus who died, now glorified, King of all kings.

81 Make me a channel of your peace

Sebastian Temple

Make me a channel of your peace,
where there is hatred let me bring your love,
where there is injury, your pardon Lord,
and where there's' doubt, true faith in you.

Make me a channel of your peace,
where there's despair in life let me bring hope,
where there is darkness, only light,
and where there's sadness ever joy.

O Master, grant that I may never seek
so much to be consoled as to console,
to be understood as to understand,
to be loved as to love with all my soul.

Make me a channel of your peace,
it is in pardoning that we are pardoned,
in giving to all men that we receive
and in dying that we're born to eternal life.

82   Mary immaculate, star of the morning   *F.W. Weatherell*

Mary immaculate, star of the morning,
chosen before the creation began,
chosen to bring, for thy bridal adorning,
woe to the serpent and rescue to man.

Here, in an orbit of shadow and sadness
veiling thy splendour, thy course thou hast run;
now thou art throned in all glory and gladness
crowned by the hand of thy saviour and Son.

Sinners, we worship thy sinless perfection,
fallen and weak, for thy pity we plead;
grant us the shield of thy sovereign protection,
measure thine aid by the depth of our need.

Frail is our nature, and strict our probation,
watchful the foe that would lure us to wrong,
succour our souls in the hour of temptation,
Mary immaculate tender and strong.

Bend from thy throne at the voice of our crying;
bend to this earth which thy footsteps have trod;
stretch out thine arms to us living and dying,
Mary immaculate, mother of God.

83   Morning has broken   *Eleanor Farjeon*

Morning has broken like the first morning,
blackbird has spoken like the first bird.
Praise for the singing! Praise for the morning!
Praise for them, springing fresh from the Word!

Sweet the rain's new fall sunlit from heaven,
like the first dew-fall on the first grass.
Praise for the sweetness of the wet garden,
sprung in completeness where his feet pass.

Mine is the sunlight! Mine is the morning
born of the one light Eden saw play!
Praise with elation, praise ev'ry morning,
God's re-creation of the new day!

84 Mother of God's living Word

Damian Lundy

Mother of God's living Word,
glorifying Christ your Lord;
full of joy, God's people sing,
grateful for your mothering.

Virgin soil, untouched by sin,
for God's seed to flourish in;
watered by the Spirit's dew
in your womb the Saviour grew.

Sharing his humility,
Bethlehem and Calvary,
with him in his bitter pain,
now as Queen with him you reign.

We are God's new chosen race,
new-born children of his grace,
citizens of heaven who
imitate and honour you.

We, God's people on our way,
travelling by night and day,
moving to our promised land,
walk beside you hand in hand.

Christ, your Son, is always near,
so we journey without fear,
singing as we walk along:
Christ our joy, and Christ our song!

Sing aloud to Christ with joy
who was once a little boy!
Sing aloud to Mary, sing,
grateful for her mothering.

85 My God loves me

v.1 Anon. v2-5 Sandra Joan Billington

My God loves me.
His love will never end.
He rests within my heart
for my God loves me.

His gentle hand
he stretches over me.
Though storm-clouds threaten the day
he will set me free.

He comes to me
in sharing bread and wine.
He brings me life that will reach
past the end of time.

My God loves me,
his faithful love endures.
And I will live like a child
held in love secure

The joys of love
as offerings now we bring.
The pains of love will be lost
in the praise we sing.

86 **My Soul is filled with joy**   *Author unknown*

My soul is filled with joy
as I sing to God my Saviour:
he has looked upon his servant,
he has visited his people.

*And holy is his name
through all generations!
Everlasting in his mercy
to the people he has chosen,
and holy is his name!*

I am lowly as a child,
but I know from this day forward
that my name will be remembered,
for all men will call me blessed.

I proclaim the pow'r of God!
He does marvels for his servants;
though he scatters the proud-hearted
and destroys the might of princes.

To the hungry he gives food,
sends the rich away empty.
In his mercy he is mindful
of the people he has chosen.

In his love he now fulfils
what he promised to our fathers.
I will praise the Lord, my saviour.
Everlasting is his mercy.

87 My soul proclaims the Lord my God

My soul proclaims the Lord my God,
my spirit sings his praise!
He looks on me, he lifts me up,
and gladness fills my days.

All nations now will share my joy,
his gifts he has outpoured;
his little one he has made great;
I magnify the Lord.

For those who love his holy name,
his mercy will not die.
His strong right arm puts down the proud
and lifts the lowly high.

He fills the hungry with good things,
the rich he sends away.
The promise made to Abraham
is filled to endless day.

Magnificat, magnificat,
magnificat, praise God!
Praise God, praise God, praise God, praise God,
magnificat, praise God!

88 Now thank we all our God   *Martin Rinkhart*

Now thank we all our God,
with heart and hands and voices,
who wondrous things hath done,
in whom this world rejoices;

who from our mother's arms
hath blessed us on our way
with countless gifts of love,
and still is ours today.

O may this bounteous God
through all our life be near us,
with ever joyful hearts
and blessed peace to cheer us;
and keep us in his grace,
and guide us when perplexed,
and free us from all ills
in this world and the next.

All praise and thanks to God
the Father now be given,
the Son, and him who reigns
with them in highest heaven,
the one Eternal God,
whom earth and heaven adore;
for thus it was, is now,
and shall be evermore.

89 Now the green blade riseth

J. M. C. Crum

Now the green blade riseth from the buried grain,
wheat that in the dark earth many days has lain;
Love lives again, that with the dead has been;
love is come again like wheat that springeth green.

In the grave they laid him, Love whom men had slain,
thinking that never he would wake again,
laid in the earth like grain that sleeps unseen:
love is come again like wheat that springeth green.

Forth he came at Easter, like the risen grain,
he that for three days in the grave had lain;
quick from the dead my risen Lord is seen:
love is come again like wheat that springeth green.

When our hearts are wintry, grieving or in pain,
thy touch can call us back to life again;
fields of our hearts that dead and bare have been:
love is come again like wheat that springeth green.

90 O bread of heaven

St Alphonsus Liguori tr. E. Vaughan

O bread of heaven, beneath this veil
thou dost my very God conceal;
my Jesus, dearest treasure, hail;
I love thee adoring kneel;
each loving soul by thee is fed
with thine own self in form of bread.

O food of life, thou who dost give
the pledge of immortality;
I live; no, 'tis not I that live;
God gives me life, God lives in me:
he feeds my soul, he guides my ways,
and every grief with joy repays.

O bond of love, that dost unite
the servant to his living Lord;
could I dare live, and not requite
such love - then death were meet reward:
I cannot live unless to prove
some love for such unmeasured love.

Beloved Lord in heaven above,
there, Jesus, thou awaitest me;
to gaze on thee with changeless love,
yes, thus I hope, thus shall it be:
for how can he deny me heaven
who here on earth himself hath given?

91 O Christ the healer

Fred Pratt Green

O Christ, the healer, we have come
To pray for health, to plead for friends.
How can we fail to be restored,
When reached by love that never ends?

From ev'ry ailment flesh endures
Our bodies clamour to be freed;
Yet in our hearts we would confess
That wholeness is our deepest need.

How strong, O Lord, are our desires,
How weak our knowledge of ourselves!
Release in us those healing truths
Unconscious pride resists or shelves.

In conflicts that destroy our health
We recognise the world's disease;
Our common life declares our ills:
Is there no cure, O Christ, for these?

Grant that we all, made one in faith,
In your community may find
The wholeness that, enriching us,
Shall reach the whole of humankind.

92 O Christe Domine Jesu *Taizé*

O Christe Domine Jesu, O Christe Domine Jesu.

93 O healing river *Traditional Baptist Hymn*

O healing river,
send down your waters,
Send down your waters
upon this land.
O healing river
send down your waters,
And wash the blood
from off the sand.

This land is parching,
this land is burning,
No seed is growing
in the barren ground.
O healing river
send down your waters,
O healing river
send your waters down.

Let the seed of freedom,
awake and flourish,
Let the deep roots nourish,
let the tall stalks rise.
O healing river
send down your waters,
O healing river,
from out of the skies.

94 O Lord, hear my prayer

Taizé

O Lord, hear my prayer, O Lord, hear my prayer,
when I call answer me.
O Lord, hear my prayer, O Lord, hear my prayer,
come and listen to me.

95 O Lord, my God

Stuart K. Hine

O Lord, my God, when I in awesome wonder,
consider all the worlds thy hand has made,
I see the stars, I hear the rolling thunder,
thy pow'r throughout the universe displayed.

Then sings my soul, my Saviour God, to thee:
How great thou art, how great thou art. (2)

And when I think that God, his Son not sparing,
sent him to die, I scarce can take it in
that on the cross, my burden gladly bearing,
he bled and died to take away my sin.

When Christ shall come with shout of acclamation
and take me home, what joy shall fill my heart;
when I shall bow in humble adoration,
and there proclaim: my God, how great thou art.

96 O Lord, you are the centre of my life

Refrain Paul Inwood

O Lord, you are the centre of my life:
I will always praise you,
I will always serve you,
I will always keep you in my sight.

Keep me safe, O God, I take refuge in you.
I say to the Lord: 'You are my God.
My happiness lies in you alone;
my happiness lies in you alone.'

I will bless the Lord who gives me counsel,
who even at night directs heart.
I keep the Lord ever in my sight:
since he is at my right hand, I shall stand firm.

And so my heart rejoices, my soul is glad;
even in safety shall my body rest.
For you will not leave my soul among the dead,
nor let your beloved know decay.

You will show me the path of life,
the fullness of joy in your presence,
at your right hand, at your hand
happiness for ever.

97   O Mary, when our God chose you   *Damian Lundy*

Oh Mary, when our God chose you
to bring his dear Son to birth,
a new creation made in you
gave joy to all the earth.

Alleluia, alleluia, alleluia, alleluia.
A new creation made in you
gave joy to all the earth.

When he was born on Christmas night
and music made the rafters ring,
the stars were dancing with delight;
now all God's children sing.

One winter's night, a heap of straw
becomes a place where ages meet,
when kings come knocking at the door
and kneeling at your feet.

In you, our God confounds the strong
and makes the crippled dance with joy;
and to our barren world belong
his mother and her boy.

In empty streets and broken hearts
you call to mind what he has done;
where all his loving kindness starts
in sending you a son.

And Mary, while we stand with you,
may once again his Spirit come,
and all his brothers follow you
to reach our Father's home.

272

98   O Mother blest, whom God bestows   *St Alphonsus Liguori*

O Mother blest, whom God bestows
on sinners and on just,
what joy, what hope thou givest those
who in thy mercy trust.

Thou art clement, thou art chaste,
Mary, thou art fair;
of all mothers sweetest, best;
none with thee compare.

O heavenly mother, mistress sweet!
It never yet was told
that suppliant sinner left thy feet
unpitied, unconsoled.

O mother pitiful and mild,
cease not to pray for me;
for I do love thee as a child,
and sigh for love of thee.

Most powerful mother, all men know
thy Son denies thee nought;
thou askest, wishest it, and lo!
his power thy will hath wrought.

O mother blest, for me obtain
ungrateful though I be,
to love that God who first could deign
to show such love for me.

99 Oh, the love of my Lord   *Estelle White*

Oh, the love of my Lord is the essence
of all that I love here on earth.
All the beauty I see he has given to me
and his giving is gentle as silence.

Every day, every hour every moment
have been blessed by the strength of his love.
At the turn of each tide he is there at my side,
and his touch is gentle as silence.

There've been times
when I've turned from his presence,
and I've walked other paths, other ways.
But I've called on his name in the dark of my shame,
and his mercy was gentle as silence.

100 Oh, the word of my Lord   *Damian Lundy*

Oh, the word of my Lord, deep within my being.
Oh, the word of my Lord, you have filled my mind.

Before I formed you in the womb
I knew you through and through,
I chose you to be mine.
Before you left your mother's side
I called to you my child, to be my sign.

I know that you are very young
but I will make you strong - I'll fill you with my word;
and you will travel through the land
fulfilling my command which you have heard.

And ev'rywhere you are to go
my hand will follow you; you will not be alone.
In all the danger that you fear
you'll find me very near,
your words my own.

With all my strength you will be filled:
you will destroy and build, for that is my design.
You will create and overthrow,

reap harvests I will sow
- your word is mine.

101 Oh when the saints

Traditional

Oh when the saints go marching in, (2)
I want to be in that number,
when the saints go marching in.

Oh when the drums begin to bang …

Oh when the stars fall from the sky...

Oh when the moon turns into blood...

Oh when the sun turns into fire …

Oh when the fires begin to blaze...

Oh when the Lord calls out the names …

102 One bread, one body

John B Foley

One bread, one body, one Lord of all.
One cup of blessing which we bless,
and we, though many, throughout the earth,
we are one body in this one Lord.

Gentile or Jew, servant or free,
woman or man, no more.

Many the gifts, many the works.
One in the Lord, of all.

Grain for the fields, scattered and grown,
Gathered to one for all.

103 Peace is flowing like a river

Anonymous

Peace is flowing like a river,
flowing out through you and me,
spreading out into the desert,
setting all the captives free.

Let it flow through me! Let it flow through me!
Let the mighty love of God now flow through me!
Let it flow through me! Let it flow through me!
Let the mighty love of God now flow through me!

Love is flowing like a river…

Joy is flowing like a river…

Hope is flowing like a river…

104 Praise, my soul, the king of heaven

Henry Francis Lyte

Praise, my soul, the king of heaven!
To his feet thy tribute bring.
Ransomed, healed, restored, forgiven,
who like me his praise should sing?
Praise him! Praise him! (2)
Praise the everlasting king!

Praise him for his grace and favour
to our fathers in distress;
praise him still the same for ever,
slow to chide and swift to bless.
Praise him! Praise him! (2)
Glorious in his faithfulness!

Father-like he tends and spares us;
well our feeble frame he knows;
in his hands he gently bears us,
rescues us from all our foes.
Praise him! Praise him! (2)
Widely as his mercy flows!

Angels, help us to adore him;
ye behold him face to face;
sun and moon bow down before him,
dwellers all in time and space.
Praise him! Praise him! (2)
Praise with us the God of grace!

105 Praise to the Holiest

John Henry Newman

Praise to the Holiest in the height,
and in the depth be praise,
in all his words most wonderful,
most sure in all ways.

O loving wisdom of our God!
When all was sin and shame,
a second Adam to the fight,
and to the rescue came.

O wisest love! That flesh and blood
which did in Adam fail,
should strive afresh against the foe,
should strive and should prevail.

And that a higher gift than grace
should flesh and blood refine,
God's presence and his very self,
and Essence all divine.

O generous love! That he who smote
in man for man the foe,
the double agony in man
for man should undergo.

And in the garden secretly
and on the cross on high,
should teach his brethren, and inspire
to suffer and die.

Praise to the Holiest in the height,
and in the depth be praise,
in all his words most wonderful,
most sure in all his ways.

106 Praise to the Lord, the Almighty

J. Neander

Praise to the Lord, the Almighty,
    the King of creation!
O my soul, praise him,
    for he is your health and salvation.

All you who hear, now to his altar draw near,
join in profound adoration.

Praise to the Lord, let us offer
    our gifts at his altar;
let not our sins and transgressions
    now cause us to falter.
Christ, the High Priest, bids us all join his feast.
Victims with him at the altar.

Praise to the Lord, who will prosper
    our work and defend us;
surely his goodness and mercy
    here daily attend us,
ponder anew all the Almighty can do,
he who with love will befriend us.

Praise to the Lord,
    oh, let all that is in us adore him!
All that has life and breath,
    come now in praises before him.
Let the Amen sound from his people again,
now as we worship before him.

107 Praise to you, O Christ our Saviour   Bernadette Farrell

Praise to you, O Christ, our Saviour,
Word of the Father, calling us to life;
Son of God who leads us to freedom:
glory to you, Lord Jesus Christ!

You are the Word who calls us out of darkness;
you are the Word who leads us into light;
you are the Word who brings us through the desert:
glory to you, Lord Jesus Christ!

You are the one whom prophets hoped and longed
for;
you are the one who speaks to us today;
you are the one who leads us to our future:
glory to you, Lord Jesus Christ!

You are the Word who calls us to be servants;
you are the Word whose only law is love;
you are the Word made flesh who lives among us:
glory to you, Lord Jesus Christ!

You are the Word who binds us and unites us;
you are the Word who calls us to be one;
you are the Word who teaches us forgiveness:
glory to you, Lord Jesus Christ!

108 Seek ye first

Karen Lafferty

Seek ye first the Kingdom of God
and his righteousness,
and all these things shall be added unto you.
Allelu, alleluia.

Alleluia, alleluia, alleluia,
allelu, alleluia.

Ask and it shall be given unto you,
seek and ye shall find.
Knock and the door shall be opened unto you.
Allelu, alleluia.

109 Shalom

Steven Jones

Shalom my friend, shalom my friend,
shalom, shalom.
The peace of Christ I give you today,
shalom, shalom.

110 Sing a new song unto the Lord

Daniel L Schutte

Sing a new song unto the Lord,
let your song be sung from mountains high.
Sing a new song unto the Lord, singing alleluia.

Yahweh's people dance for joy,
oh come before the Lord
and play for him on glad tambourines,
and let your trumpet sound.

Rise, O children, from your sleep,
your Saviour now has come,
and he has turned your sorrow to joy,
and filled your soul with song.

Glad my soul, for I have seen the glory of the Lord.
The trumpet sounds, the dead shall be raised,
I know my Saviour lives.

111 Sing it in the valleys

Mike Anderson

Sing it in the valleys, shout it from the mountain tops;
Jesus came to save us, and his saving never stops.
He is King of Kings, and new life he brings,
Sing it in the valleys, shout it from the mountain tops; (Oh!)
shout it from the mountain tops!

Jesus, you are by my side, you take all my fears.
If I only come to you,
you will heal the pain of years.

You have not deserted me, though I go astray.
Jesus take me in your arms,
help me walk with you today.

Jesus, you are living now, Jesus I believe.
Jesus take me heart and soul,
yours alone I want to be.

112 Sing of a girl in the ripening wheat

Damian Lundy

Sing of a girl in the ripening wheat,
flow'rs in her hand, the sun in her hair.
All the world will run to her feet
for the child that mother will bear.

Sing of a girl that the angels surround,
dust in her hand, and straw in her hair.
Kings and their crowns will fall to the ground
before the child that mother will bear.

Sing of a girl on a hillside alone,
blood on her hand, and grey in her hair.

Sing of a body, broken and torn.
Oh, the child that mother will bear!

Sing of the girl a new man will meet,
hand in his hand, the wind in her hair.
Joy will rise as golden as wheat
with the child that mother will bear.

Sing of a girl in a cirle of love.
fire on her head, the light in her hair.
Sing of the hearts the spirit will move
to love the child that mother will bear.

Sing of a girl who will never grow old,
joy in her eyes and gold in her hair.
Through the ages men will be told
of the child that mother will bear.

113 Sing of Mary. pure and lowly

Roland F. Palmer

Sing of Mary. pure and lowly,
virgin mother undefiled.
Sing of God's own Son most holy,
who became her little child.
Fairest child of fairest mother,
God, the Lord, who came to earth,
Word made flesh, our very brother,
takes our nature by his birth.

Sing of Jesus, son of Mary,
in the home at Nazareth.
Toil and labour cannot weary
love enduring unto death.
Constant was the love he gave her,
though he went forth from her side,
forth to preach and heal and suffer,
till on Calvary he died.

Glory be to God the Father,
glory be to God the Son;
glory be to God the Spirit,
glory to the three in one.

From the heart of blessed Mary,
from all saints the song ascends
and the Church the strain re-echoes
unto earth's remotest ends.

114 Sing of the Lord's goodness

Ernest Sands

Sing of the Lord's goodness
Father of all wisdom,
come to him and bless his name.
Mercy he has shown us, his love is for ever,
faithful to the end of days.

Come then all you nations,
sing of your Lord's goodness,
melodies of praise and thanks to God.
Ring out the Lord's glory,
praise him with your music,
worship him and bless his name.

Power he has wielded,
honour is his garment,
risen from the snares of death.
His word he has spoken,
one bread he has broken,
new life he now gives to all.

Courage in our darkness,
comfort in our sorrow,
Spirit of our God most high;
solace for the weary,
pardon for the sinner,
splendour of the living God.

Praise him with your singing,
praise him with the trumpet,
praise God with the lute and harp;
praise him with the cymbals,
praise him with your dancing,
praise God till the end of days.

115 Sing to the mountains

Bob Dufford

Sing to the mountains, sing to the sea.
Raise your voices, lift your hearts.
This is the day the Lord has made.
Let all the earth rejoice.

I will give thanks to you, my Lord,
You have answered my plea.
You have saved my soul from death.
You are my strength and my song.

Holy, holy, holy Lord.
Heaven and earth are full of Your glory.

This is the day that the Lord has made.
Let us be glad and rejoice.
He has turned all death to life.
Sing of the glory of God.

116 Song of Farewell

Ernest Sands

May the choirs of angels come to greet you;
may they speed you to paradise.
May the Lord enfold you in his mercy;
may you find eternal life.

The Lord is my light and my help;
it is he who protects me from harm.
The Lord is the strength of my days;
before whom should I tremble with fear?

There is one thing I ask of the Lord;
that he grant me my heartfelt desire.
To dwell in the courts of our God
ev'ry day of my life in his presence.

O Lord, hear my voice when I cry;
have mercy on me and give answer.
Do not cast me away in your anger,
for you are the God of my help.

I am sure I shall see the Lord's goodness;
I shall dwell in the land of the living.
Hope in God, stand firm and take heart,
place all your trust in the Lord.

117 Soul of my Saviour

Ascribed to John XXII

Soul of my Saviour, sanctify my breast;
Body of Christ, be thou my saving guest;
Blood of my Saviour, bathe me in thy tide,
wash me with water flowing from thy side.

Strength and protection may thy Passion be;
O Blessed Jesus hear and answer me;
deep in thy wounds, Lord, hide and shelter me;
so shall I never, never part from thee.

Guard and defend me from the foe malign;
in death's dread moments make me only thine;
call me, and bid me come to thee on high,
when I may praise thee with thy saints for aye

118 Spirit of the living God

Michael Iverson

Spirit of the living God, fall afresh on me.
Spirit of the living God, fall afresh on me.
Break me, melt me, mould me, fill me.
Spirit of the living God, fall afresh on me.

119 Sweet sacrament divine

Francis Stanfield

Sweet sacrament divine,
hid in thy earthly home,
lo! round thy lowly shrine,
with suppliant hearts we come;
Jesus, to thee our voice we raise,
in songs of love and heartfelt praise,
sweet sacrament divine. (2)

Sweet sacrament of peace,
dear home of every heart,
where restless yearnings cease,
and sorrows all depart,
there in thine ear all trustfully
we tell our tale of misery,
sweet sacrament of peace. (2)

Sweet sacrament of rest,
Ark from the ocean's roar,
within thy shelter blest
soon may we reach the shore,
save us, for still the tempest raves;
save, lest we sink beneath the waves
sweet sacrament of rest. (2)

Sweet sacrament divine,
earth's light and jubilee,
in thy far depths doth shine
thy Godhead's majesty;
sweet light, so shine on us, we pray,
that earthly joys may fade away,
sweet sacrament divine. (2)

120 Take our bread

Joseph Wise

Take our bread, we ask you,
take our hearts, we love you,
take our lives, O Father, we are yours, we are yours.

Yours as we stand at the table you set;
Yours as we eat the bread our hearts can't forget.
We are the signs of your life with us yet:
We are yours, we are yours.

Your holy people stand washed in your blood,
Spirit filled yet hungry we await your food.
Poor though we are,
we have brought ourselves to you
We are yours, we are yours.

121 The Church's one foundation

S. J. Stone

The Church's one foundation,
is Jesus Christ, her Lord;
she is his new creation,
by water and the word;
from heav'n he came and sought her
to be his holy bride,

with his own blood he bought her,
and for her life he died.

Elect from every nation,
yet one o'er all earth,
her charter of salvation
one Lord, one faith, one birth;
one holy name she blesses,
partakes one holy food,
and to one hope she presses,
with every grace endued.

'Mid toil, and tribulation,
and tumult of her war,
she waits the consummation
of peace for evermore;
till with the vision glorious
her longing eyes are blest,
and the great Church victorious
shall be the Church at rest.

Yet she on earth hath union
with God the Three in one,
and mystic sweet communion
with those whose rest is won:
O happy ones and holy!
Lord, give us grace that we
like them, the meek and lowly
on high may dwell with thee.

122 The day thou gavest

John Ellerton

The day thou gavest, Lord, is ended:
the darkness falls at thy behest;
to thee our morning hymns ascended;
thy praise shall sanctify our rest.

We thank thee that thy Church unsleeping,
while earth rolls onward into light,
through all the world her watch is keeping,
and rests not now by day or night.

As o'er each continent and island
the dawn leads on another day,
the voice of prayer is never silent,
nor dies the strain of praise away.

The sun that bids us rest is waking
our brethren 'neath the western sky
and hour by hour fresh lips are making
thy wondrous doings heard on high.

So be it, Lord; thy throne shall never,
like earth's proud empire, pass away;
thy kingdom stands, and grows for ever,
till all thy creatures own thy sway.

123 The King of love my shepherd is

H. W. Baker

The King of love my shepherd is,
whose goodness faileth never;
I nothing lack if I am his
and he is mine for ever.

Where streams of living water flow
my ransomed soul he leadeth,
and where the verdant pastures grow
with food celestial feedeth.

Perverse and foolish oft I strayed
but yet in love he sought me,
and on his shoulder gently laid,
and home, rejoicing, brought me.

In death's dark vale I fear no ill
with thee, dear Lord, beside me;
thy rod and staff my comfort still,
thy cross before to guide me.

Thou spread'st a table in my sight,
thy unction grace bestoweth:
and O what transport of delight
from thy pure chalice floweth!

And so through all the length of days
thy goodness faileth never;
good Shepherd, may I sing thy praise
within thy house for ever.

124 The Lord hears the cry of the poor

John B. Foley

The Lord hears the cry of the poor.
Blessed be the Lord.

I will bless the Lord at all times,
his praise ever in my mouth.
Let my soul glory in the Lord,
for he hears the cry of the poor.

Let the lowly hear and be glad:
the Lord listens to their pleas;
and to hearts broken he is near,
for he hears the cry of the poor.

Ev'ry spirit crushed he will save;
will be ransom for their lives;
will be safe shelter for their fears,
for he hears the cry of the poor.

We proclaim the greatness of God,
his praise ever in our mouth;
ev'ry face brightened in his light,
for he hears the cry of the poor.

125 The Lord is my light

Taizé

The Lord is my light,
my light and salvation:
in him I trust, in him I trust.

126 The Lord's my shepherd

Scottish Psalter

The Lord's my shepherd, I'll not want,
he makes me down to lie
in pastures green. He leadeth me
the quiet waters by.

My soul he doth restore again,
and me walk doth make
within the paths of righteousness,
e'en for his own name's sake.

Yea, though I walk in death's dark vale,
yet will I fear none ill.
For thou art with me, and thy rod
and staff me comfort still.

My table thou hast furnished
in presence of my foes,
my head thou dost with oil anoint,
and my cup overflows.

Goodness and mercy all my life
shall surely follow me.
And in God's house for evermore
my dwelling-place shall be.

127 The love I have for you, my Lord

Carey Landry

The love I have for you, my Lord,
is only a shadow of your love for me;
only a shadow of your love for me;
your deep abiding love.

My own belief in you, my Lord,
is only a shadow of your faith in me;
only a shadow of your faith in me;
your deep and lasting faith.

My life is in your hands;
my life is in your hands.
My love for you will grow , my God.
Your light in me will shine.

The dream I have today, my Lord,
is only a shadow of your dreams for me;
only a shadow of all that will be;
if I but follow you.

The joy I feel today, my Lord,
is only a shadow of your joys for me
only a shadow of your joys for me;
when we meet face to face.

My life is in your hands;
my life is in your hands.
My love for you will grow , my God.
Your light in me will shine.

128 The Spirit lives to set us free

The Spirit lives to set us free,
walk, walk in the light.
he binds us all in unity
walk, walk in the light.

Walk in the light,(3)
walk in the light of the Lord!

Jesus promised life to all,
The dead were wakened by his call.

He died in pain on Calvary,
to save the lost like you and me.

We know his death was not the end.
He gave his Spirit to be our friend.

By Jesus's love our wounds are healed.
The Father's kindness is revealed.

The Spirit lives in you and me
His light will shine for all to see.

129 This day God gives me

James Quinn SJ

This day God gives me strength of high heaven,
sun and moon shining flame in my hearth,
flashing of lightning, wind in its swiftness,
deeps of the ocean, firmness of earth.

This day God sends me strength as my steersman,
might to uphold me, wisdom as guide.
Your eyes are watchful, your ears are listening,
your lips are speaking, friend at my side.

289

HYMNS

God's way is my way, God's shield is round me,
God's host defends me, saving from ill.
Angels of heaven, drive from me always
all that would harm me, stand by me still.

Rising, I thank you, mighty and strong One,
King of creation, giver of rest,
firmly confessing Threeness of persons,
Oneness of Godhead, Trinity blest.

130 This is my body (In love for me)   *Jimmy Owens*

This is my body, broken for you,
bringing you wholeness, making you free.
Take it and eat it, and when you do,
do it in love for me.

This is my blood, poured out for you,
bringing forgiveness, making you free.
Take it and drink it, and when you do,
do it in love for me.

Back to my Father, soon I shall go.
Do not forget me; then you will see
I am still with you, and you will know,
you're very close to me.

Filled with my Spirit, how will you grow,
you are my branches; I am the tree.
If you are faithful, others will know,
you are alive in me.

Love one another - I have loved you,
and I have shown you how to be free:
serve one another, and when you do,
do it in love for me.

131 This is the day   *Author unknown*

This is the day, (2)
that the Lord has made, (2)
We will rejoice, (2)
And be glad in it, (2)

This is the day, that the Lord has made,
we will rejoice, and be glad in it!
This is the day (2)
that the Lord has made!

This is the day,
when he rose again ...

This the day,
when the Spirit came ...

132 This is what Yahweh asks of you   *Mary McGann, RSCJ*

This is what Yahweh asks of you, only this:
that you act justly, that you love tenderly,
that you walk humbly, with your God.

'My children, I am with you such a little while,
and where I go now you cannot come.
A new commandment I give to you:
as I have loved you, so love each other.'

'Do not let your hearts be troubled;
trust in God now, and trust in me.
I go to prepare a place for you,
and I shall come again to take you home.'

'Peace is the gift I leave with you,
a peace the world can never give.
If you keep my word, my Father will love you,
and we will come to you to make our home.'

133 Though the mountains may fall   *Daniel L. Schutte*

Though the mountains may fall,
and the hills turn to dust,
yet the love of the Lord will stand
as a shelter for all who will call on his name.
Sing the praise and the glory of God.

Could the Lord ever leave you?
Could the Lord forget his love?

Though a mother forsake her child,
he will not abandon you.

Should you turn and forsake him,
he will gently call your name.
Should you wander away from him,
he will always take you back.

Go to him when you're weary,
he will give you eagle's wings.
You will run, never tire,
for your God will be your strength.

As he swore to your fathers,
when the flood destroyed the land.
He will never forsake you,
he will swear to you again.

134 Ubi Caritas

Taizé

Ubi caritas et amor, ubi caritas Deus ibi est.

135 Unless a grain of wheat

Bernadette Farrell

*Unless a grain of wheat shall fall
upon the ground and die,
it remains but a single grain
with no life.*

If we have died with him then we shall live with him;
if we hold firm we shall reign with him.

If anyone serves me then they must follow me;
wherever I am my servants will be.

Make your home in me as make mine in you;
those who remain in me bear much fruit.

If you remain in me and my word lives in you;
then you will be my disciples.

Those who love me are loved by my Father;
we shall be with them and dwell in them.

Peace I leave with you, my peace I give to you;
peace which the world cannot give is my gift.

136 Wait for the Lord

Taizé

Wait for the Lord, his day is near,
Wait for the Lord, be strong take heart.

137 Walk with me

Estelle White

Walk with me, oh my Lord,
through the darkest night and brightest day.
Be at my side, oh Lord,
hold my hand and guide me on my way.

Sometimes the road seems long,
my energy is spent.
Then, Lord, I think of you
and I am given strength.

Stones often bar my path
and there times I fall,
but you are always there
to help me when I call.

Just as you calmed the wind
and walked upon the sea,
conquer, my living Lord,
the storms that threaten me.

Help me to pierce the mists
that cloud my heart and mind
so that I shall not fear,
the steepest mountain-side.

As once you healed the lame
and gave sight to the blind,
help me when I'm downcast
to hold my head up high.

138 Water of Life

Stephen Dean

Water of life, cleanse and refresh us;
raise us to life in Christ Jesus.

All you who thirst, come to the waters,
and you will never be thirsty again

As rain from heav'n, so is God's word,
it waters the earth and brings forth life.

Dying with Christ, we shall rise with him,
death shall no longer have pow'r over us;

Turn to the Lord, cast off your wickedness,
you will find peace in his infinite love.

139 We are the Easter People

Tom Leigh

We are the Easter People: 'Alleluia!' is our song.
Let us rejoice! Let us sing out: 'Jesus is risen!'
Alleluia! Alleluia! Alleluia!

He died for us: now he is risen:
we share his life: Jesus is Lord!

His light shines out, dispelling the darkness.
Tell the whole world: Jesus is Lord!

Proclaim his glory: Christ is the Saviour.
He dies no more: Jesus is Lord!

God's people sing! You share his victory.
Have no more fear: Jesus is Lord!

140 When I survey the wondrous cross

Isaac Watts

When I survey the wondrous cross
on which the Prince of Glory died,
my richest gain I count but loss,
and pour contempt on all my pride.

Forbid it, Lord, that I should boast,
save in the death of Christ, my God:
all the vain things that charm me most,
I sacrifice them to his blood.

See from his head, his hands, his feet,
sorrow and love flow mingled down;
did e'er such love and sorrow meet,
or thorns compose so rich a crown?

Were the whole realm of nature mine,
that were an offering far too small;
love so amazing, so divine,
demands my soul, my life, my all

141 Will you come and follow me

Kelvin Grove

Will you come and follow me
If I but call your name?
Will you go where you don't know
and never be the same?
Will you let my love be shown,
will you let my name be known,
will you let my life be grown
in you and you in me?

Will you leave yourself behind
if I but call your name?
Will you care for cruel and kind
and never be the same?
Will you risk the hostile stare
should your life attract or scare?
Will you let me answer prayer
in you and you in me?

Will you let the blinded see
if I but call your name?
Will you set the prisoners free
and never be the same?
Will you kiss the leper clean,
and do such as this unseen,
and admit to what I mean
in you and you in me?

Will you love the 'you' you hide
if I but call your name?
Will you quell the fear inside
and never be the same?

Will you use the faith you've found
to reshape the world around,
through my sight and touch and sound
in you and you in me?

Lord, your summons echoes true
when you but call my name.
Let me turn and follow you
and never be the same.
In your company I'll go
where your love and footsteps show.
thus I'll move and live and grow
in you and you in me.

142 Yahweh, I know you are near

Daniel L. Schutte

Yahweh, I know you are near,
standing always at my side.
You guard me from the foe
and you lead me in ways everlasting.

Lord you have searched my heart,
and you know when I sit and when I stand.
Your hand is upon me protecting me from death,
keeping me from harm.

Where can I run from your love?
If I climb to the heavens, you are there.
If I fly to the sunrise or sail beyond the sea,
still I'd find you there.

You know my heart and its ways,
you who formed me before I was born,
in secret of darkness, before I saw the sun,
in my mother's womb.

Marvellous to me are your works;
how profound are your thoughts, my Lord!
Even if I could count them, they number as the stars,
you would still be there.

143 You shall cross the barren desert

Robert J. Dufford

You shall cross the barren desert,
but you shall not die of thirst.
You shall wander far in safety,
though you do not know the way.
You shall speak your words to foreign men,
and they will understand.
You shall see the face of God and live.

Be not afraid, I go before you always.
Come, follow me, and I will give you rest.

If you pass through raging waters
in the sea, you shall not drown,
If you walk amid the burning flames,
you shall not be harmed.
If you stand before the power of hell
and death is at your side,
know that I am with you through it all.

Blessed are the poor,
for the kingdom shall be theirs.
Blest are you who weep and morn,
for one day you shall laugh.
And if wicked men insult and hate you
all because of me,
blessed, blessed are you.

144 You who dwell (On eagles wings)

Michael Joncas

You who dwell in the shelter of the Lord,
who abide in his shadow for life,
say to the Lord: 'My refuge,
my rock in whom I trust!'

And he will raise you up on eagles' wings,
bear you on the breath of dawn,
make you to shine like the sun,
and hold you in the palm of his hand.

The snare of the fowler will never capture you,
and famine will bring you no fear:
under his wings your refuge,
his faithfulness your shield.

You need not fear the terror of the night,
nor the arrow that flies by day;
though thousands fall about you,
near you it shall not come.

For to his angels he's given a command
to guard you in all of your ways;
upon their hands they will bear you up,
lest you dash your foot against a stone.

INDEX OF HYMNS, SONGS & REFRAINS

Acknowledgements

The publishers wish to express their gratitude to the following for permission to use copyright material in this book. If any errors or omissions have occurred these will be corrected in future editions.

Texts:

The English translation of the Roman Missal © 1973, Rite of Anointing and Pastoral Care of the Sick © 1982, International Committee on English in the Liturgy, Inc. (ICEL)

The Scripture quotations contained herein are from the New Revised Standard Version Bible: Catholic Edition copyright 1989 by the Division of Christian Education of the National Council of the Churches of Christ in the USA. Used by permission. All rights reserved.

Psalm texts from *The Psalms, A New Translation* © 1963 The Grail (England) published by Harper Collins in Fontana Books.

Photographs:

HCPT & Simon Simon Archer, Photo Durand, Photo Viron,

Hymns:

1 © 1974 Shalom Community, 1504 Polk, Wichita Falls, Texas 76309. USA.

2,17,28,69,70,92,94,125,134,136, © Ateliers et Presses de Taizé

3 © Robertson Publications Stockley Close, Stockley Rd, West Drayton, Middx UB7 9BE

4,5,11,18,21,25,27,33,37,40,42,51,52,56,60,65,66,84,97,100,112,128,139,85 © Kevin Mayhew Ltd. Reproduced by Permission from Hymns Old & New

7,81 © Franciscan Communications & New Dawn Music

9 © Word of God/Copycare Ltd

12,19,39,58,110,133,142 Daniel L. Scutte and New Dawn Music

14,16,20,29,36,53,62,73,77 © Kingsway's Thankyou Music

15 © 1985 Christopher Walker. Published by OCP Publications.

23 © 1972 The Benedictine Foundation of the State of Vermont, Inc.

30 © Chevalier Press, PO Box 13, Kensington, NSW 2033, Australia

31,32108 © Maranatha Music/Copycare Ltd

35,63,102,134 John B Foley SJ and New Dawn Music

41,130 © Bud John Songs/Fine Balance Music. Administered by Copycare

45 © Search Press, Wellwood, North Farm Rd, Tunbridge Wells, Kent TN2 3DR

ARRR

ACKNOWLEDGE

RELATE IT

RECEIVE FATHER

RESPONSE

GOD APOINT ME WILL ANOINT ME